Recognition
Rebooted

Recognition Rebooted

Sam Jenniges, M.S.

Cover design by Michelle Fairbanks, Fresh Design
Book composition by Lori Hughes, Lori Hughes Publishing Services
Graphics by Alicia Bauer, Ally B Designs, and Michelle Fairbanks, Fresh Design
Editing by Liz Thompson, House Style Editing, and
    Lori Hughes, Lori Hughes Publishing Services
Proofreading by Julie Grady, Grady Editorial Services

ISBN-13: 978-1-73361-831-1

Library of Congress Control Number: 2019902195

Second Edition: May 2019
First Edition: March 2018

To my parents, Alphonse and Elaine,
thank you for being the first to show recognition for valuable work.
Your balance of doing the right thing and breaking a few rules
has been priceless.

To my home team, Dan, Olivia, Benjamin, and Simon,
my favorite travel companions and mentors,
I am so grateful for your love, laughter, and
ever-present ridiculous nonsense.

Contents

Why This Book?

If you are fortunate, your manager recognizes the value you deliver and tells you about it. Most of us, however, are not so lucky and might occasionally find that our managers left a gift card or a company-branded item on our desks, but we don't specifically know why. When appreciation for your work is communicated *well* and *directly* to you, the associated feeling rushes straight to your heart and mind, along with a healthy dose of dopamine. Employee recognition does the business good, too.

Studies of authentic employee recognition have shown that:

- teams who receive praise increased their productivity by 31%,[1] and
- managers nationwide[2] who center on their employees' strengths can essentially eliminate active disengagement and double the average of those who are engaged (reaching full potential).

Yet 65% of North American employees report that their work wasn't recognized *a single time* during the previous year.[3] What's more, according to another study, employees who feel their work is unrecognized *are twice as likely* to quit their jobs within the year.[4]

Billions of dollars are spent on employee recognition, with most of those dollars having no impact on the organization's performance. There is a major disconnect between organizations and managers believing they recognize employees and their employees actually feeling appreciated.

And no wonder: Managers across the globe lack training in recognition delivery and have even been unfairly expected to be "naturals" at recognition. In fact, only 14% of companies provide the necessary tools and training for recognition delivery.[5] Since people leave organizations largely because of their relationships with their

> "We do a lot with employee recognition, but as with a lot of companies, it isn't always seen that way by employees."
> —*Executive of an international health services organization*

managers, one of the skills a manager *needs* is the ability to sincerely recognize and appreciate work well done.

I wrote this book because the more I researched and spoke with leaders (and colleagues and friends and strangers in the coffee shop), the more compelled I became to determine why something that can be so simple and that can have such a big payoff for both employees and employers is, at best, scarcely and ineffectively (and, at worst, dysfunctionally) delivered across most organizations.

Recognition Rebooted invites you to rethink the outdated notions of employee recognition and rewards for a smarter, more deliberate, and effective approach. For every leader who influences the work of others, this book will address the costly and preventable lack of effective recognition delivery, and includes tools you can use starting *today*.

Using two main characters in a fictitious business allows us to imagine how recognition works in most businesses (i.e., well-intentioned but ineffective) and how a few purposeful and thoughtful changes can improve both morale and productivity.

Let's cut the noise and misconception out of this terrifically important management responsibility and *opportunity*. You'll find it makes a real difference to your team's attitude and performance, which ultimately affect your bottom line.

Introduction

When many of us think about employee recognition, our first thought is about what reward we might purchase for a particular employee. This isn't surprising: Recognition is estimated to be a $46 billion market, with 87% spent on tenure rewards,[6] though such rewards have little impact on an organization's performance. This means that:

1. our reward-driven recognition programs are largely powered by the people deciding the budget rather than by a supervisor with direct knowledge of the employee's performance, and
2. our decision to recognize our employees often starts with whether or not we have a budget to do so.

Rather than focusing on an effective approach to recognizing work well done and feeding our employees' intrinsic motivation, we seem to blindly rely on external rewards to motivate our teams. It's not working. In spite of the many and varied recognition (reward) systems in place across organizations, research has found that:

- only 32% of the U.S. population is fully engaged at work[7] and only 13% worldwide,[8] and
- 70–84% of employees are job hunting at any given time.[9]

Highlighting the ineffectiveness of existing recognition (reward) programs, 75% of organizations have a recognition program, but 58% of their employees aren't aware it exists.[10]

Why then, since recognition impacts employee performance and retention, do we often miss key opportunities to foster loyalty and to grow our number of high-performing team members? Something is wrong. Employee recognition is either not occurring effectively or, more typically, not taking place at all.

As a manager, you will impact 70% of your employee's engagement experience.[11] *You* have more influence on your team's performance than anyone else in the organization. That's good news! Yet, for most of us, recognition doesn't come naturally. Our intentions are good, but successful, effective recognition delivery is difficult without recognition tools and training. Leadership and management are woven together. Of course, managers must plan, organize, find efficiencies, and so on. They show *leadership* by inspiring, influencing, and developing others, which helps increase retention and performance. In short, you are *practicing* true leadership when you are providing recognition as part of everyday interactions with your team.

Your employees want to be recognized for work well done. Because providing such recognition is at the heart of being a great leader, your business will benefit, and you and your team will notice measurable results.

Why Recognition Matters

Moving Up and Over

"So it's true, then?"

Mark glanced up as he placed a stack of file folders into his moving box and replied, "Hey David, so what's true?"

"That no matter how far up we move in the organization we never escape the stacks of paper."

"I'm not gonna lie—sometimes we just need to see the paper version."

Looking at the piles of folders, binders, and books in Mark's office, David said, "Apparently heaps of it."

"Don't be a judger; though I will say that every time I pack up my office, I do a little purging. So, unless I can restrain myself, I fully expect to replace all of it and more, in my new job."

That sounded about right for David, too. He walked over to the bookshelf to lend a hand with the packing and offhandedly remarked, "I still think it was very big of Donna to help you move up and over to a different division."

"Yeah, what can I say? It was something about the benefit to the organization, my career growth, my skills. . . . Shall I go on?"

Rolling his eyes, David said, "You know, it gets lonely being the sole witness to this *charming* side of you. But before you can interrupt me, back to my point that Donna is one excellent boss! She's got the organization's back and your back, and she knows that helping you advance helps elevate her career. Us. You. Me. It's the working person's trinity, really."

"A winning combination for sure. It did take her some time to find her people-management stride, but you know Donna, a quitter she is not! I've learned from her leadership growth, and I've bene-fited from her unending support. And with her clout, it is paying off for the trinity, as you call it."

"I'm just not so sure I'd be as mature as she is about letting my team member move on, even if it is across the hall," laughed David.

"Sure you would."

"Yes, of course, I would."

"I honestly feel ready for this role, the level of leadership, and the challenges that I know will come with it. Transitioning these past few weeks has seriously helped me go in with eyes wide open. And this weekend, I plan to recharge my batteries before I dive *all in* on Monday. First thing I'll do after I get up tomorrow. . . ."

"Whoa, cool! You still have this!" interrupted David holding a small notebook in his hand.

Shifting his thoughts from recharging before Monday, Mark looked more closely at what David was holding up. "Of course, I still have it. I may have forgotten where I put it, but yeah, it's a keeper!"

David leafed through the familiar notebook as Mark quickly walked around his desk to look over his shoulder. With each page, they were reminded of the employee recognition ideas that the two of them uncovered three years ago. "Amazing what a little curiosity, a willing co-worker, and a notebook can accomplish," reflected David.

Giving them a mental pat on the back, Mark thought of Donna's support, the influence that he, David, and his manager peers have had on their teams' retention and performance, not to mention his own career. The notebook reminded him of how proud he was about living these recognition concepts he so deeply believed in.

Pointing to a page, David blurted out, "How about this page? The Essential TIPSS! I use these all the time when I recognize my team! It's cool to revisit the original pages."

Mark wistfully added, "I can still speak to them like we were delivering the training only yesterday." Without peeking, he proceeded to recite the Recognition Delivery Essential TIPSS and then, glancing back at the notebook, validated each one.

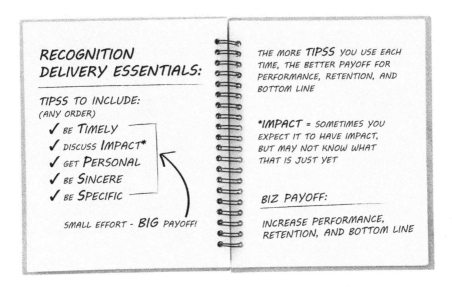

"The TIPSS are one of my favorite concepts; they're so practical. I like things that are doable and easy to remember," David said after reading them.

"Well, it's impossible for me to choose a favorite child from the notebook, but I will say I never met an acronym I didn't like. No shame in wanting things to be easy!"

Moving on, David said, "How about our Recognition Fundamentals here? We were feeling pretty bold about challenging some traditional notions of recognition."

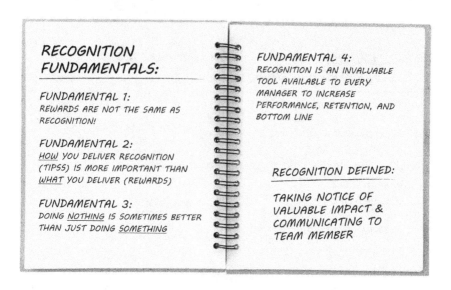

"True. It's great to see that these stand the test of time. I'm proud of how these Fundamentals helped drive our recognition approach as a company and as individual managers. And they still do."

"We packed a lot of information into these two notebook pages," David remarked. "And it took us a while to decide on them."

Mark recalled a little about their process and how they arrived at these four Recognition Fundamentals. His thoughts began rolling back to their countless conversations about these concepts and the others they developed. "A lot of meetings, observations, and strong coffee!" he concluded.

Like Mark, David also scanned his thoughts and wondered to himself: *What started the whole recognition conversation and why did we create this notebook to begin with?* "The setback that occurred with Team Donna: that was our beginning, wasn't it?" he asked Mark.

"It was a tough time for our department. And yes, that really was what triggered our employee recognition conversations."

"And triggered the notebook, and the training, *and* your book. And while we're at it, is your book packed away yet?"

"Shucks! You're embarrassing me," Mark told him. "I have a few on the middle shelf near you."

David pulled one of Mark's books off the shelf and said, "You have to feel pretty good about this. I mean the notebook tracked our concepts, and you wrote a book about it!"

"Team effort! And I do continue to feel good about it. It's been really enjoyable to see it used here. The feedback is so gratifying."

"The book also helped test the four Recognition Fundamentals and Essential TIPSS. It helped many things and still does," said David as he put the book into a moving box. Thinking back to the original thought of what started this recognition conversation, David opened the notebook again and flipped through more of the pages. A slow grin crossed Mark's face and setting the packing aside, he and David began to revisit from the beginning the story and their recognition discoveries.

★ ★ ★ ★ ★
Three Years Earlier

Team Donna

Since her promotion to vice president at Bensi Corp three years ago, Donna remains intensely focused on running the Hard-lines Department of the Merchandising Division. She spends a great deal of time planning and poring over the numbers, fore-casting, and generating reports and presentations for her boss to help ensure organizational strategic decisions.

She was handed a smaller stagnant department called Gold-lines, to oversee as well. An unusual step for her division, but there is great confidence that Donna has the skills and eagerness to grow it into an earnest department similar to what she is doing for Hardlines. With her responsibilities in strategy, growth planning, and researching as well as her availability to her team so they can do their jobs well, is there ever a night that she doesn't work? Her team jokes with her that, if it wasn't for her interest in traveling, she might never take a break. In spite of what could seem a relentless schedule, Donna thrives on the work and what is required of her. She loves the responsibility and the hard-won success that Hardlines has seen so far.

A major win for Donna this year is her idea of prototyping smaller storefronts in highly populated urban areas. Her research showed the storefront idea as a high potential for the risk, and the executive team and board agreed. If successful, the results of this experiment will contribute considerably to their competitive market.

Career growth is vital, and Donna works hard to move her team to their next level. The more they grow in their jobs, the more their departments can produce. It is rewarding, working on the moving parts of the puzzle, just a bit more research and benchmarking to be sure. She is eager to dive into another book she saw on the business bestseller list that will inform her planning, or at least help her stay on top of her industry reading. She jotted down a reminder to get the link to her team for their reading lists.

Donna can see that after just 18 months in his role as manager of the analysts, Mark already has the leadership skills and drive to advance his career. She feels so fortunate that he transferred to her team from the Marketing/PR/Sales Department. Donna admires how much Mark's team respects him and how they consistently perform. He continues to seek more senior-level responsibilities, and she expects to increase his paygrade this year.

She knows he wants to advance his career, but for now, Mark expressed that in his current role, there is plenty of room for significant business and leadership growth. He eagerly grows his skills within an existing role to the highest potential before moving on. That is ideal for Donna. She wants someone in the role who can advance without moving out of the department too soon. Mark seems to enjoy leading and directing his team of individual contributors—something that will change if he has designs on a more executive role in the future. She appreciates how easily and often Mark has initiated career conversations with her and as a result, she never really has to ask him what he wants out of his career.

Ajay, her senior buyer and peer to Mark, is less descriptive about what he wants from his current role and career, even though he could be the company example of someone moving up in the organization quickly. He has earned it. Career conversations with him aren't as built into their regular meetings as they are with Mark—partly because Mark initiates the topic and partly because Ajay likes to keep his options open, as he says. As long as he keeps growing and advancing, he seems to be happy. That works great for Donna since her succession planning points to Ajay filling her own vice president role someday.

When they talked about Ajay's career path six months ago, he seemed energized by advancing, so she continues to give him high-level assignments whenever possible. He would do things differently from Donna if, and when, he is in her role, and she finds that especially healthy. Donna's idea to prototype smaller storefronts is an area where Ajay can offer unique contributions beyond what Mark and his team are helping with. She appreciates Ajay initiating ideas as he has done with the prototyping plan. He has other ideas that would help, but for now, it is working out great and he continues to be very productive directly impacting the bottom line.

Donna wishes she had more time to work with Ajay to figure out how his other ideas and suggestions about workflow fit into what they are doing. Eventually, she will find time to make more room for those less urgent but important things, not just with Ajay but with her team. She is too busy meeting her quarterly goals to focus on that now. Besides, they agreed that he would let her know if he needs more from her.

Donna's two key leaders seemed to be in their stride working well together and delivering results. The department is well positioned to meet its goals with these two capable leaders on her team. They will be enormously helpful as she focuses on her own career growth. Her experience and promotions through the Softlines Department, now her counterpart department, have prepared her well for her role as Hardlines vice president. As long as she continues to deliver—and Ajay and Mark will be instrumental in that—the senior leaders will support finding ways for her to advance in her role. Her team is doing many things right, as proven with the success of Hardlines.

One thing is for sure: Donna is not going to run (or *not* run) her department like her peer Stephen does in Softlines. His two key managers are virtually leaderless. She doesn't envy his team, but a part of her wonders how he pulls it off. He doesn't seem to do anything, yet assumes the credit for his team. He's the only leader she knows who can delegate his entire day-to-day job. The Softlines Department has always been neck-and-neck with hers financially.

She wonders if that will persist beyond this year when Stephen joined the company.

She has noticed some turnover on his team. Stephen never breaks a sweat—even when his team manager left six months ago, David filled that role quickly. Maybe Stephen being absent from his team is what saves them. She can't imagine the damage he could do to a team if he were in their business. The clients love him, though, and senior executives aren't rocking *that* boat. She'll give him credit for that!

Afford the Exceptional: Bensi Corp

Bensi Corp is growing fast. The online business has exploded in the past five years and has complemented and boosted the existing storefront business. Since its inception 22 years ago, Bensi Corp has continued to find ways to stay competitive in the market and, in the past decade, to achieve a global presence. The recent shift in strategy to 75% online and 25% storefront has kept it agile and impressively competitive with the big box stores as well as the competitive online commerce companies.

The past few years have shown confidence in consumer spending, and the 15,000 employees at Bensi Corp continue to deliver on their "Afford the Exceptional" promise.

Customers have responded well to the business model of the three major retail lines existing in the Merchandising Division.

1. Hardlines, led by Donna, the nonapparel merchandise known as hard goods, includes electronics, furniture, sporting equipment, and so on.
2. Softlines, led by Stephen, are items such as linens, sportswear, and a clothing line with accessories. These "soft goods" have also historically done well.
3. The third line, Goldlines, was absorbed into the Hardlines Department and are the "in between" goods such as seasonal supplies.

The original storefront in Minneapolis continues to be central to the brand while remaining in the black. Bensi Corp plans to add approximately 1,000 more employees globally over the next three years. Its managers will need to continue to retain and hire exceptional employees to fulfill Bensi Corp's growth plans to expand their offerings and market share.

Magic Mark

It didn't take long for the news of Ajay's resignation to make its way around the Merchandising Division. David picked up his phone and began tapping into it.

> DAVID: I'm feeling Donna's pain about Ajay leaving.

> MARK: Me too. I can tell it's weighing on her.

> I was surprised yet not, when he resigned.

> Same.

> Have you talked to him?

> I did. Made me stop calling him Golden Child.

> Thought you two already had that little talk.

Long time ago, but you know he has a gazillion ideas, sees things uniquely, gets stuff done...

So when he told me, I lost all sense, and then regressed.

This is a regrettable loss.

True, but it sounds like a good opportunity for him.

It really is. He has opps here too though, but I got a restless vibe from him last few weeks. Put feelers out with him, but he wasn't forthcoming.

Did Donna get that vibe?

She will need to understandably balance "I saw it coming yet didn't stop it" with "I was very surprised and admit taken off guard."

Yes. This will pass, people do leave orgs, happens all the time.

Good to keep perspective. It will feel personal to Donna and it will be hard to replace his caliber. So, double whammy thing going on for her.

Yup. She seems hard on herself. But you will do what we usually do for these roles, find replacement and play to strengths.

We will...

...But we are a good team darn it! (If I could somehow convey a little whining with that, I surely deserve to.)

You two are Donna's dream team. (Consider said whining conveyed.)

It's going to be hard to witness my favorite mentor relive what she could have done differently. It's what she'll do you know.

I was gonna say 'it's what we would all do' but then I rapidly thought of my boss and my role and NOPE!

I don't see Stephen spending even ten seconds wondering if he could have done something differently if I resigned.

His leadership distance was the appeal for taking the job at this point in my career. Knew his skills lay, er ah, elsewhere, and I could just do my thing and make a difference. It's a perfect yet unsustainable partnership. For now, I'm okay with that.

...Are you even listening?

Half-heartedly. My mind is on more pressing issues like my department and getting through this with minimal impact.

More pressing than me??? (Don't answer that—I would then have to agree with you)

Go work your magic. Donna will appreciate your leadership assist.

Getting my cape now.

There Goes a High Performer

Ajay had the attention of the executive team early on—and not just in the Merchandising Division. His savvy business and relationship skills helped him work his way up from an analyst to a manager to a buyer and finally a senior buyer of the Hardlines Department rapidly—within four years. No one was a quicker study than Ajay. While most retail strategies focus largely on cyberworld growth, with Donna's support he was instrumental in the preparation and heavy-lifting needed for Bensi Corp to consider the viability of prototyping small storefronts. It was said that he would take Donna's role eventually, though the timeframe of that was vaguely in the future. His departure was a big surprise to almost everyone.

Donna had intended to talk with Ajay about career progression at their annual career development conversation. It would be an appropriate time to see if he was fulfilled in his current role, especially with the challenging projects he had helped with. Now it was too late.

Now that her colleagues are aware of Ajay's resignation, some of them would know what had been making her sick for the past week since she has learned from Ajay of his decision. His leaving will hurt the Hardlines business. Finding a senior buyer for Hardlines may take time, but that's not the punch in the gut. People leave organizations all the time, even capable, respectable, amazing employees like Ajay. It's not that he is leaving; it's that she didn't find a way to help him stay. She didn't find a way to help the *previous* manager stay. Ajay was her second key manager in the past three years—two too many—who have moved on to other organizations. She is concerned about her business and how this will look for the team and is questioning her leadership skills. If Donna is honest with herself, she turned a blind eye to what her gut was telling her when the previous manager resigned. Now this time, she ignored the signs that Ajay was seeking other opportunities.

When she asked, he told her he found a great opportunity that he couldn't pass up. It's what they will all say. Which will be true. Partly. But why leave if he had promising opportunities here?

Ajay got an increase in pay and even got an unexpected bonus this year. Plus, his annual work anniversary gift. So many people would love to have that. Why wasn't that enough for Ajay? He did tell her how grateful he was for those things; still, he moved on. He seemed excited about the new role, and she wonders if there is more to it than that. She was hoping the bonus and anniversary gift would make him happy. Even though Ajay may not admit it, if she were writing his exit interview, it would probably say something like: While he could see his eventual career path, he wasn't clear when or where he could advance.

If she had initiated more conversations about that, maybe she could have even prevented his resignation. Donna knows there are lessons to take to heart here, but for now, she is focused on how to minimize the loss to her business, find his replacement, and keep Hardlines buyers on track.

Ajay didn't intend to leave Bensi Corp, but he was intrigued when a friend told him about an exciting role at the company where she worked. He loved how he moved up at Bensi Corp and how Donna believed in his work and continued to drive results forward. He also knew that if he wanted to wait around—not sure how long—that a more senior role might be his.

Ajay did feel a little frustrated that there wasn't a lot of energy or encouragement focused on exploring new ideas. In hindsight, he supposes he could have pushed that further, especially since he believes that is where he could add unique value. Being a little frustrated seemed okay with him until he interviewed for his new job. His intention was just to see what it was all about.

Updating his resume and preparing for the interview became more and more energizing as he listed his contributions to Bensi Corp and the results that he and his team had delivered. The interviewer was very astute in identifying the impact Ajay had made at Bensi Corp, something Ajay didn't generally discuss with external people. His focus at Bensi Corp was primarily on ensuring deliverables most effectively and often in inventive ways. This wasn't about running from Bensi Corp, but rather finding something better where he knew his work, and the role itself, would get more explicit visibility. Still, it was not easy to leave the organization that helped him grow his career.

* * * * *

Why Don't We Recognize Our Team Members More Often?

Moving quickly to replace Ajay as senior buyer, Donna hired Laura, an internal transfer, within three weeks. While understanding that it will take time for Laura to perform at peak level and being very realistic about Ajay performing at a uniquely high level, Donna and Mark were content with her skills and how rapidly she was hired. They believe that, with her experience, Laura will eventually offer her own set of skills to Hardlines.

MARK: I am so pleased with myself.

DAVID: You figured out which biz books get your attention this month?

That was decided weeks ago. You underestimate me.

Yet I expect this is not why you are pleased with yourself.

Not today.

Grabbing coffee. Meet me downstairs if you have a few – you can fill me in.

Perfect – see you in 5.

After a few minutes, David waved Mark over to his table where he had placed two black coffees for the two of them.

"Okay, what's this about? Ajay? Is this about easing Donna's mind? Your new hire, or what?"

"Donna and I chatted briefly about his resignation, and she shared some of her deep thinking, not just about Ajay, but the previous manager who left too. You know Donna; she will not let this go until she can figure out how to prevent it in the future. She mentioned she would turn to research for some answers about turnover and loyalty in general. It was a good conversation, and she seemed to feel better with having an immediate plan. So, while she's taking it hard and owns this, she is as professional and gracious as always. *And*, we are both relieved, not to mention highly confident, with Laura as his replacement."

"You are fortunate to have Laura join the team, I understand."

"We are. However, what I am more interested in right now is sharing a great moment I had with one of my team members."

"Don't keep me in suspense!"

"It was one of those awesome times! She performed so incredibly well under a tight timeline with a high-pressure focus on quality. Not an easy combination."

David frowned slightly and admitted, "I've got that ugly punch-in-the-gut-comparison-feeling just now, but go on. Never mind me."

Ignoring David's insecurity, Mark continued, "Thank you for that 'never mind me' out. I'm actually talking about that feeling of knowing when an employee did well by *your team*, that extra step, beyond what was asked of her and the fact that she is driven to do well. I'll just say it: It makes me so proud."

"Must have been especially noticeable given the staffing turmoil at Hardlines with the Ajay exit. I imagine that you and Donna have been pushing everyone hard in addition to looking for his replacement."

"Yes, made it all the more awesome. When I notice a team member doing well, it feels like I get a buzz just by acknowledging that to the person. Honestly, this is when I love being a manager most," Mark said, leaning back leisurely in his chair. Popping forward, he continued, "You know when I love my job the least?"

"Don't do it . . ."

"When I don't acknowledge my team's contributions. And get stuck on what they are *not* doing. It's like saying you're sorta valued here sometimes. Like my brain is drawn to what's wrong and not what's right."

"I hear you, and yet you couldn't bask in your small glory today?"

"Apparently not."

David did know what Mark meant and thought to himself that managers are hardwired to look for what's *not* working. They need to *fix* things.

Mark wondered, "So if it can feel like a little buzz, why don't most of us recognize our employees more? Are we too focused on being *managers* where you fix things versus *leaders* where you are *also* looking at what's going well?"

"Hmm, good questions." After some thought, David said, "I believe I am supposed to know how to recognize my employees properly, but when I think about it, I spend so much mental energy that I usually just end up avoiding it. I'm not sure about the reward process: deciding and then shopping for the reward and then doing the paperwork. For me, employee recognition just ends up being too much guessing and time. It's not a reasonable excuse, but if I'm honest, that is what holds me back. There, I said it. How's that for leadership?"

"That sounds like something many of us might say. Unsure, energy gets bogged down in the process, so much easier to just avoid it," Mark said.

"Although, when I have recognized employee performance in the past, I handed out movie tickets at the staff meeting. The team loves them, of course, but then I can't help thinking about three of my top performers getting what everyone else got. That doesn't feel right either. For the ones who take extra steps, I felt a little guilty for not recognizing their work more, or differently. When I look back, one person specifically, might have been performing at a C+ grade and not improving. In fact, thinking further, sending the blanket message to everyone for the same job really watered it down. Giving all employees the same recognition, or rewards really, is fairly common now that I think about it more."

Mark jumped in, "I think so. We both have been on that receiving end of *blanket* rewards, and you miss the chance to recognize each person based on that individual's contribution. Or *non*contribution. It's like letting the rewards do the talking!"

"Well said!"

Mark ventured, "Managers may be underserved in the area of recognition guidance or training. Your point of not being sure how to recognize hits the nail on the head."

"I'm here to say that it isn't natural for most of us managers. I am living proof."

"It also seems to have gotten unnecessarily complicated. Which is probably why we often end up doing nothing," Mark added.

"For me, it's not that I don't think recognition is important, I just feel that I don't know the best way to deliver it in a way that doesn't feel awkward, but is more real. But, when I remember, I do let people occasionally know when they do a good job."

They both concluded that there is a lot to be said about recognition delivery. Mark asked that they catch lunch the following week and talk more about it. "I have a lot of interest around this, and it would be great to sort out my thoughts."

That sounded good to David who was in deep thought. "I am wondering if these are the only reasons managers don't recognize. They are unsure how and feel awkward."

"I wonder too. What do you think about asking Jan? It's been six months since you've worked with her. It would be interesting to hear her take on why we don't recognize our teams more."

David added that his peer Jan, the senior buyer, seems underwater and her team appears to reflect that with some of the turnover. "I wonder if Jan would say her reason is that she doesn't have time."

"I wonder if that might be a common answer too. I'm going to check with other peers. I'm officially inspired now to hear what barriers or obstacles we might learn about."

David stood up and said, "I'm glad we're talking about this. I know my team could use some recognition and I want to make sure I continue on great footing with them."

"Sounds good. I am on my way to recognize my analyst right now. If the conversation goes as I think it will, we will both feel a shot of adrenaline."

"I want some of that!" David grabbed the rest of his coffee and started toward his office and shouted, "Enjoy the rush; let's catch lunch next week!"

Donna's Employee Recognition Data

Hindsight and backpedaling—that's where Donna knows she will spend some time. The conversation with Mark was very helpful in taking the next steps in what she might do to prevent key resignations, if possible. When Mark shared some thoughts about his and David's preliminary employee recognition conversations, it revived those warning signs she had ignored with Ajay.

How many times have they pushed past the present wins of their department to relentlessly focus on what's next, without acknowledging the value of those wins? How many of Ajay's ideas had she brushed aside because they didn't seem to fit with her order of thinking even though her gut said they were valuable? Her team knows that her responsibility is to run a successful department— and she has been. They are always talking about getting to the next level and staying successful as a department. *They have to know how grateful I am for their dedication; we even mentioned it at our annual meeting.* Should she be doing more? Probably, but what?

With Ajay leaving, Donna knows she can't afford to lose another crucial person in her department. Hiring Laura for Ajay's replacement was a win, but it will take her awhile to get up to speed as a senior buyer. Laura can offer good insight from her previous companies in addition to her internal Bensi Corp experience in Marketing/PR/Sales.

Mark says he's solid and is motivated by what he's learning. And even though they are peers, he also enjoys mentoring Laura, thankfully. Donna will never admit it to others, but she appreciates the easy connection she has with Mark. Besides Mark being very capable as a manager in Hardlines, she enjoys their great partnership. They learn a lot from each other, with Donna showing Mark the business ropes and Mark often being the sensible mirror for her. It especially helped that he was a sounding board after Ajay's decision. His insight has been so beneficial to her. He is a good friend.

Data. Donna's comfort zone. Is there data that can provide some insight? That night, at home, Donna revisited their annual Employee Engagement Survey. She was proud of her survey results as a leader. Her team expressed pride in working at the organization; she scored well as a manager in that employees feel respected, and in that she can see what their goals are and what their career steps could be. Her lowest ratings, however, were related to employees feeling valued or recognized for the work they do. While not terribly low, this has been consistent the past five years with her personal ratings as well as organization wide. When she compares with the overall results of Bensi Corp, her scores line up with other managers. Not ideal, but most are good ratings.

Being lined up to the overall corporation results is comforting to Donna, but her competitive nature wants to be one of the top-scoring managers, and it nags at her each year when the survey comes out. She is very proud that Mark, while not perfect, has higher ratings than she has, year after year. He has proven very credible with his peers and team. He's got the personality that makes people naturally respect and enjoy him, and he has extremely high expectations of his team. He scores higher than other managers in

employees feeling valued and recognized. Ajay's scores were consistently good each year. She also sees that David's ratings have
steadily increased over the years. That probably helped him win
this new role in Softlines. David seems to be becoming more skilled
as a manager. Or maybe Stephen is savvy enough to know he can
kick back even more now. Or maybe Mark is rubbing off on David.
Maybe all those things.

One thing that stood out was both her and Bensi Corp rating
lower on the question about employees feeling valued or recognized for the work they do. Picking up on some earlier industry
research, she started perusing the topic of turnover in organizations, and one thing jumped out at her: Turnover is directly related
to those mediocre scores in the area of feeling work is not valued
or recognized. That makes sense. Interestingly, she uncovered the
following research that inspired further thinking.

- Only 32% of the U.S. population is engaged at work[7] and
  only 13% worldwide.[8]

*These are disturbing statistics. This means only one-third of the
population feels that they have the opportunity to do what they do best
each day, that development is encouraged, and that their opinions count.
I do okay, though the category of "not having the opportunity to do their
best every day," may apply to Ajay. He had lots of opportunities, but did
I encourage him to do what he did best, and did I tell him the value of
those things?*

- Only one in three U.S. workers strongly agree that they
  received recognition or praise for doing good work in the
  past seven days.[4]
- At any given company, it's not uncommon for employees
  to feel that their best efforts are routinely ignored.[4]
- Employees who do not feel adequately recognized are
  twice as likely to say they'll quit in the next year.[4]

Oh dear, this is hitting close to home with Ajay.

- Companies that scored in the top 20% for building a
  "recognition-rich culture" actually had 31% lower voluntary turnover rates.[6]

Promising. It's good to know there are some possible solutions.

- 65% of Americans report receiving no praise or recognition in the past year. Few organizations give their managers the tools and training they need to provide recognition to their people.[3]

Not sure where I stand with knowing how to recognize employees. I thought I was doing okay with it, especially in the annual performance reviews and the anniversary rewards, and I remember to say "thank you" to my team regularly.

- Praise from managers was rated the top motivator for performance, beating out other noncash and financial incentives by 67%.[12]

Need to explore that more.

- Managers who focus on their employees' strengths can practically eliminate active disengagement and double the average of U.S. workers who are engaged nationwide.[2]

Wow!

And Donna realized from her research that she is not alone; most managers want to be effective, and their self-esteem is impacted by their own performance.

She wondered if maybe her first task is to see how she can participate in the company's recognition program to improve in that area. She made a note to give Human Resources (HR) a call this week to discuss.

After a late night, Donna stopped at Bensi Corp's Cuppa Kiosk first thing in the morning to meet with the HR representative. During their brief conversation, Donna learned that Bensi Corp's recognition program was developed about eight years ago in response to the lower employee engagement survey ratings in feeling valued and recognized in the workplace. They both acknowledged that the survey trend for the past five years, in the rating of feeling valued and recognized, had not improved. Donna and the HR representative wondered why there hadn't been more improvement considering Bensi Corp had implemented a robust recognition program that included Platinum, Gold, Silver, and Bronze levels.

She also learned that only a small percentage of managers and employees take advantage of the company recognition program. After thinking a little more about the recognition program at Bensi Corp and her conversation with HR, she did a little more searching and found other studies.

- Nearly 75% of organizations have a recognition program; only 58% of employees are aware that their organizations have recognition programs.[10]

Hmmm . . . sounds familiar.

- Organizations with effective recognition programs had a 31% lower voluntary turnover than organizations with ineffective recognition programs.[10]

I wonder what an effective recognition program is?

- Tenure-based rewards systems have virtually no impact on organizational performance. Of the $46 billion market for employee recognition, 87% is spent on tenure-based rewards.[6]

No impact on performance? This makes me pause since service awards seem to be the main form of recognition that I have seen. Are we rewarding longevity regardless of performance?

Donna continued her research around employee recognition, which she found fascinating if not surprising. There were several more data points she will send to Mark in light of his and David's recent conversations.

Donna realized that Mark doesn't seem to use their recognition program and yet he rated pretty high in this area. She wondered if Mark and David's recognition concepts are already working with Mark's team. He said that he isn't using the recognition program. Is this part of why he and David are doing a deeper dive into recognition? So they can more effectively deliver recognition to their teams? Donna made a note to talk with Mark more about that next time when she will also share the information she has learned.

What Recognition Is
and What It Isn't

Recognition Defined

With a long week of day-to-day operations and month-end reporting finally out of the way, it was nice to leave the office a little earlier on Friday. Before meeting, Mark and David both thought it was time to decide on a definition for authentic recognition. They agreed to think about it and meet up for a quick beer at their usual haunt, The Village Growler.

Mark flagged David down to join him at a small table. They chatted a little about the week and decided to stay for only about an hour. Mark had a busy weekend planned with several friends, and David had a full weekend of coaching his youngest daughter's soccer team.

Pulling out a notebook, Mark said, "I've been thinking about our recognition conversation . . ."

"I see a notebook. With notes. And numbers. They look almost like statistics. You've been doing more than thinking about our conversation."

"I like being prepared for profound ideas," Mark told him.

"You know, we used to go for a beer just to catch up and shoot the breeze."

Not waning in enthusiasm, Mark continued, "Besides, Donna didn't waste time on turnover and employee recognition research. She found some interesting stuff and shared it with me. Those are the stats you see in this notebook. I'll share more with you, but get this, straight from our conversation about managers being expected to just know how to recognize their teams . . ."

"I'm all ears."

"Good because this involves you! One stat Donna uncovered is that only 14% of organizations provide managers with the necessary tools for recognition. So, for something so impactful, a very small percentage of managers receive training or other tools and most are expected to be naturals."

"Interesting! And believable. What else you got for stats?"

"This one hit Donna hard: Employees who do not feel adequately recognized *are twice as likely* to say they'll quit in the next year. She thought she was recognizing Ajay very well by giving him challenging and interesting assignments, which is partly true, but there wasn't a lot of acknowledgment of the actual value of the work. I reminded her that she doesn't know that is why Ajay left. He may have just gotten a great opportunity. But Donna wonders now what more she could have done in that area."

"It seems clear that not being recognized may cause people to leave their jobs; at least it's a major reason. Is recognition really a motivator for performance? Logically when people feel positive or appreciated, I would think they would be motivated to be more productive. Certainly, I am. Anything on connecting the dots on performance?"

"Okay, we are diving in. Yes. Lots of science to back up *why* it's important from a performance perspective too." Glancing at his notes, "Donna shared this gem: Managers who recognize their teams see a substantial increase in productivity—one study claimed 31% better—than managers who were less positive and open with praise for their team. That's just one study; there are more."

"So bottom line: Let's not forget the enormous cost it takes to recruit, train, and acclimate new hires after people leave organizations."

"The combination of these stats is powerful."

"Yup, managers are not trained, and employees are not receiving appreciation, or in other words, recognition. Yet, with recognition, the data points to increased retention and performance. This is a big deal!"

"Exactly. We were right when we thought there was an underserved need for managers. Which really motivates me to explore this more."

"Okay. I may already regret it, but I told Rebecca about our conversation and our plan to pursue more thoughts about recognition. She says that you are becoming my recognition mentor," David said, motioning air quotes.

"I completely and blindly agree with that sensible woman," laughed Mark.

"Fine, but I'm not calling you my mentor."

"You can thank me later. Seriously, if it helps to remind you, I learned so much from you prior to you getting me into Bensi Corp years ago. The scorecards that help me with reports for Donna are so impactful, for example. So, are we done with the pride thing now?"

"Well, never, but let's go ahead and get our beers," suggested David.

Armed with a Guinness each and a bowl of peanuts, they felt ready to define recognition. They batted around a few thoughts on what recognition is at its core. Mark jotted it down in the notebook.

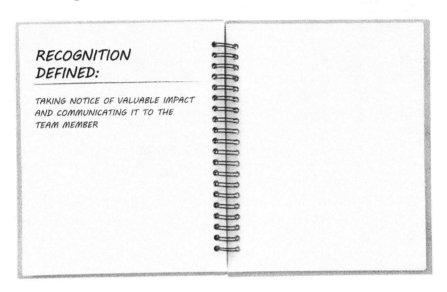

RECOGNITION DEFINED:

TAKING NOTICE OF VALUABLE IMPACT AND COMMUNICATING IT TO THE TEAM MEMBER

"I'm surprised it wasn't a little more difficult to define," said David.

"It's not that big of a mystery! We are here to *simplify*. That's what I like about this; it doesn't have to be, nor should it be, complicated! Neither of us wants recognition to be about praising someone's performance whether it had value or not. We really want to get managers recognizing strong performance."

"Yes! Otherwise, it's like getting a trophy for coming in last. As a kid, I eventually wised up to it not meaning much. And it didn't exactly motivate me to try harder if I'm getting a trophy either way. The trophies that meant something were the ones we *earned*. The recognition message should be similar: earned, because your work had valuable impact," summarized David.

"So, let's not water this down by recognizing mediocre work. That is just sad. Maybe even nauseating."

"I'm with you on the mediocre work thing; not so much on sad and nauseating. It does make me wonder: What if it's mediocre or lackluster work, yet improving, moving the needle slowly. "A for effort" sort of thing. Do we still recognize the person?"

"Right! We should clarify. Mediocre work *without* full potential: no recognition. A judgment call by the manager."

"Makes sense to me. What about mediocre work *with* full potential?"

"I say, recognize the person's effort, not their work since it isn't likely impactful."

"And if you do recognize the effort, which would be a way of encouraging progress, it should be done privately."

"*Yes!* Public recognition, in this case, would be risky and even confusing to team members if they are not in awe of the work either."

"This, of course, begs more exploration on public recognition, but let's do that later. I want to continue our thoughts on defining who gets rewarded."

After a little more discussion, they clarified that even if the work is great, if it doesn't have valuable impact or isn't aligned to priorities, then it's not a candidate for recognition. Mark said, "For example, if someone spent hours and hours modifying, say, an internal website that was arguably beautiful and even more functional but came at the expense of higher job priorities, then it would send the wrong message to the person, the team, and the organization, to recognize the work."

"Agree, so let's be clear about valuable impact then; it means great work and has impact. We aren't saying it has to be earth-shattering, right?" David went on, "I'm thinking the work itself can be broadly defined. Doesn't always mean something tangible is produced."

This inspired a spirited discussion about being recognized for small things versus making a major organizational impact. While the major organizational impact is inarguably important to recognize appropriately, Mark and David are also betting on the impact recognition can have on the less visible, yet impactful things team members may do every day beyond meeting their priorities.

"For example, an impactful idea for the department might be a book recommendation that was a game changer for someone . . . ," began Mark.

"A document that was beyond expected, or someone offering to mentor a new team member and saving a lot of headache for the manager. Lots of little things that can have a big impact in making a difference in the employee feeling appreciated."

Mark didn't want to lose sight of the communication part of the definition. "There are also things to consider when we say 'communicating it to a team member' so let's make sure we talk about that later." First, he wanted to add a few of their thoughts on the page so that they wouldn't forget.

With a little underlining and a few notes from their conversation, Mark added the following with David's input.

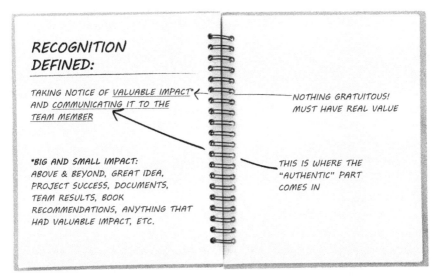

"There are many options for delivering recognition to a team member. The communication is where the *real* difference can be made and where it becomes truly authentic," said Mark.

"Totally agree."

"Communication is where a manager can shine!"

"Totally agree."

"This is also when lives are saved."

"That's a tall order and a little dramatic."

Not completely conceding, Mark carried on, "Well, hearts, minds, and careers rejuvenated at the very least anyway. Think about it. When someone you respect tells you why your work is valuable, is that not the thing you tell Rebecca when you get home?"

David immediately nodded, "When my work impacts some-thing and gets noticed, it's very motivating. Truth be told, it hasn't occurred within the last six months with Stephen. But when I have had my work recognized in the past, it makes me really proud, and it's the first thing I tell my wife when I see her."

"I believe it!"

Keeping it simple is exactly what David liked about this. But something was bothering him. "Are we being too idealistic?"

Mark responded, "Maybe we are, but it's important. I think ide-alism is a major element in driving positive change. It's energizing. It keeps the eye on the prize. But you are right; we still need to be realistic."

"True on all counts." He wanted to be realistic and talk scal-ability. "We can sit here all day talking about how easy this is—sorta—with our dozen direct reports. But some managers have dozens of people reporting to them. They could be recognizing their employees all day long. It's a lot easier for you and me. The varying team sizes and diversity in age, culture, work backgrounds, and more, make it all the more important to treat this individually. Of course, it's more effort, but a diverse team is what really helps the team performance in the long run. Different perspectives and view-points and all that. So more than ever, there is no one-size-fits-all to recognition."

"Remember, I lived it to some degree before coming here. That's why we need to help managers think about recognition as *easy to do*, making it easy to make it a habit and part of regular conversa-tions," Mark said.

"Easy is good; life has enough moving parts! I wanna hear more about the easy part."

"Okay," replied Mark. "Let's go back to rewards. If every time I want to tell someone that they did an amazing job, I have to fill out a form or shop for a reward or figure out my budget and so on, I'm not going to do it very often at all. It's too much work. Making it part of everyday conversation is a lot easier. And, managers need to learn how to do that with more ease."

"Agree. How?"

"One thing that worked for me in the past was, before an indi-vidual standing meeting with my team members, I try to think of one thing that they did in those past two weeks that had valuable impact. It makes a difference in everyone performing better, including me. And gosh darn it! It feels good to let the good stuff see the light of day!"

David replied, "That's an easy idea. I like it. It may not, however, be realistic if you have a team member who is not performing very strongly."

"Agree. It depends on why they are underperforming. Are they new to the task, or do they have attitude issues? Recognition for low performers is worth further conversation. Let's pick that up later."

Getting out his pen, David said, "Yup, let's. I also want to capture Key Take-Aways from our conversation. I think we have a few from this conversation as well as earlier. He wrote the following in the notebook.

OTHER KEY TAKE-AWAYS:

✓ MANAGERS FOCUS ON FIXING THINGS; LEADERS ALSO FOCUS ON WHAT'S GOING WELL.

✓ FOR MEDIOCRE PERFORMANCE WITH FULL EFFORT, RECOGNIZE EFFORT VS THE WORK. (PRIVATELY)

✓ BEFORE INDIV. MEETINGS, ESPECIALLY WITH HIGH PERFORMERS, TELL THEM ONE THING THAT THEY DID THAT HAD VALUABLE IMPACT.

Recognition for Performance

Finding a table at Oliva's Café across the street, Mark and David picked up where they left off a week ago.

"I hope that you can recognize your own team's valuable impact in your role at Softlines. It may not be completely understood or easy with Stephen, but you are finding that out," Mark commented.

"Well, as I've said before, I did take this role with eyes wide open. I knew that the reason Bensi Corp brought Stephen on board last year was for his client relationships. And that is his singular focus, for better or worse. But knowing that, I felt prepared and haven't been too surprised."

"Good."

"I see a chance to help motivate Jan, peer to peer. My observation in the past six months is that she's holding her own as our senior buyer. I can't help but believe that if she and I could be on the same page, we could help each other manage Stephen, or at least support each other to be a stronger peer team."

"The research Donna shared really does make a case for the bottom line being a big-deal reason for recognition. It's like saying rain and sunshine make the grass grow."

"Most of us can agree with that. But I've been thinking more about our recognition conversations, and you gotta know that my current focus as a manager is learning my new job, planning, finding efficiencies, establishing processes, earning the credibility of learning the industry, accomplishing quarterly goals—you get the picture. I'm not sure I have a lot of time to pursue recognition just now."

Mark, getting more serious, said, "I know you're busy and being credible at your job is a must; I get it. Recognition falls flat if, as a manager, you are failing in your own goals or in understanding the industry and are not respected by your team. It doesn't replace good management skills like communication, planning, budgeting, goal setting, and so forth. I still want to keep discussing recognition, though, when you can carve out some time, because I see it as an integral part of my job in developing my team, not something we do in isolation of our role."

"It still takes time to recognize."

"Yup. But I think it's easier than most of us think. More importantly, you can plug away at your efficiencies and your goals, but doing that without the leadership component leaves a lot out. The more we provide recognition as part of regular interactions with your team, the more our leadership skills improve."

"I can see that benefit."

Wasting no time, Mark continued, "I want to focus on recognition for performance specifically. You know, what we've been talking about. I also want to share with you another email Donna sent." Mark shared the $46 billion recognition market statistic and where most of the dollars are spent. "Basically, most of the money is spent on tenure awards that have no impact. And it's not impacting anything significant."

"I'm shocked. And in many cases, it may be a reward for just sticking around regardless of how well the person is performing. Is that the message we want to send? You can see where this can get muddled. Performance recognition seems to be lumped in with things like years of service or retirement or a major family event. You know, things that are not above and beyond, but milestones that get recognized."

"So service awards should be simply to acknowledge and even celebrate undisputable milestones. They should have little to do with performance and should not be in place of employee recognition," said Mark.

"Recognition is for strong performers or above-and-beyond performance—work that has valuable impact—versus an everyone-gets-a-trophy kind of mentality."

"Yes."

"I want to solidify recognition for valuable performance in an authentic and uncomplicated way. That's what I believe managers need help with."

"That's what *I* want help with! Except it brings up more stuff I have done wrong in the past," said David.

"Me too, and I'm glad you can laugh about it. Though I like the idea of service awards being separate from recognition for performance."

"Separating those sounds right to me, but let's focus on the larger need of delivering recognition for valuable performance. Honestly, I feel that sometimes the service awards too often take the place of recognizing actual performance. Wonder how many people experience service awards the way that I had in one company.

We would get a catalog when an anniversary came up and could choose a gift based on the parameters they gave us. Of course, I should be happy to get the gift, but it's very impersonal and it came from corporate, so no one really acknowledged my service anniversary in any meaningful way."

"I know that occurs in other companies. And I'm sure it would have meaning if additional recognition took place for performance," said Mark.

"Exactly, and, unlike my previous company with my rockstar manager, it did not. So, I say, keep on keepin' on with service awards, if that's where you want your dollars to go and you believe it is impactful, but for the love of Pete at least look people in the eye and thank them! For our purposes, let's focus on the higher payoff: recognition for performance."

Mark continued, "Now that we know our focus and we already have our definition, let's also talk about what recognition isn't, who gets recognized, stuff like that."

"Oh good! I see more painful reminders of my past mistakes. Why not carve out time for another conversation?"

"That's the spirit!"

Caution! Public Recognition Ahead

The quarterly department meeting led by the senior vice president, Sebastian, who was Donna and Stephen's direct manager, included the usual discussion of goal progress with a celebration on the agenda. The meeting ended with Sebastian handing out $25 gift cards to all 24 people in the Hardlines Department. He wanted to recognize them for beta testing the new customer software and working around the clock with quality and skill in parallel with the existing system.

MARK: Whatcha think?

DAVID: Good meeting. My second in this division.

How about the recognition part?

Just spit it out!

Okay, but I get credit for giving you a chance...

The mtg confirms something you triggered during one of our conversations about recognition & rewards.

I think we may be thinking the same thing.

I'm grabbing another coffee. Can you meet me at Cuppa Kiosk and let's chat while fresh on mind. 20 min tops! My turn to buy.

Okay because I have a crazy afternoon.

Mark got their coffees and spotted a private space at a tall, pub-like table near a window where David joined him.

Mark started with his reaction from the quarterly meeting. "First of all, the meeting was really nice. Nice to see people be publicly recognized even though it was a systemized approach and one-size-fits-all. And delivered by someone who isn't close to the work. And it was from six weeks ago."

The way he put it, the meeting didn't sound nice at all. David also noticed some gaps.

"I couldn't help but observe the celebration part," said Mark. "This approach might be fine, but I did wonder if employees experience other recognition during the year from their manager, besides what they received from Sebastian today."

"Good question."

"If not, it's flat. Not authentic. I don't mean to be critical; it just points out the need for more awareness around recognition. And similar to what we talked about earlier, not everyone pulled the same weight during the beta testing. I'm pretty sure that any team is keenly aware of who does and who does not pull their weight. So, everyone getting the same recognition and rewards could be demotivating for those who worked to their potential."

"It reminds me of group projects back in school. The ones who worked hard to make sure the project went well got a raw deal compared with those who did little and still got the same grade."

"The one-size-fits-all is so ingrained," added Mark.

"And the beta testing example is similar; you can see how it could cause resentment or bitterness for their team members. So, I wonder then, if public recognition should even be done?"

"That isn't what I'm saying. It seems fine to do and even good. It's just that this one was front-loaded with the reward. The gift card *was* the recognition. And did you see Robert and a few others? It did not look like they enjoyed walking up in front of others like that."

David defended that Sebastian did comment about the beta testing work and *why* they were getting the gift card. So, he was specific and spoke to the overall impact.

"I agree, but there was a *missed opportunity* to really show the value and make it more personal to each person, especially since some didn't contribute significantly to the impact."

"That would take all day," David countered.

"Yes, if you complicate it. Look, Sebastian doesn't know what people went through. So it's a generic thank you from a senior officer. Far better for Donna and me to publicly recognize them with Sebastian witnessing it, don't you think? We shake the hands of our people and thank them genuinely, and then Sebastian thanks them."

"Small difference; more personal. And senior VP sees it all," David agreed.

"Right. Simple. Personal. Doesn't address one-size-fits-all, though."

"I know you have more to say . . ."

"Do you think that after the division meeting and after everyone got their rewards, will we as managers in Hardlines check off the recognition box in our minds as a recognition-done-deal for who knows how long?"

"Honestly, I think so for most." David immediately visualized a huge caution sign hanging in front of the words "public recognition." "Is there room in that flashy notebook for a few cautionary thoughts on public recognition?"

They summarized their thoughts, and David wrote the following cautions about public recognition.

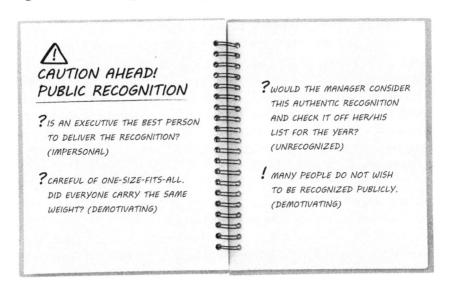

CAUTION AHEAD!
PUBLIC RECOGNITION

? IS AN EXECUTIVE THE BEST PERSON TO DELIVER THE RECOGNITION? (IMPERSONAL)

? CAREFUL OF ONE-SIZE-FITS-ALL. DID EVERYONE CARRY THE SAME WEIGHT? (DEMOTIVATING)

? WOULD THE MANAGER CONSIDER THIS AUTHENTIC RECOGNITION AND CHECK IT OFF HER/HIS LIST FOR THE YEAR? (UNRECOGNIZED)

! MANY PEOPLE DO NOT WISH TO BE RECOGNIZED PUBLICLY. (DEMOTIVATING)

"So public recognition with caution and thought. Is that our conclusion?" David asked.

It seemed like a good summary to Mark. "I've never come away from a celebration similar to this one feeling as though my work was *personally* valued. Mostly, I came away thinking it was great to get $25 bucks, and it was acknowledged that I did something. While that isn't a bad thing, I find it lacking. And that approach certainly wouldn't impact my performance or my wanting to stay, or not stay, with a company."

"So public recognition is better for the true one-size-fits-all. For example, service awards, work anniversaries, or family events but not related to performance. Yes, I like that distinction now that I've heard it out loud," said David.

"I like it too, but again, proceed with caution. Some people don't want public recognition. Some do. Let me take one group, Millennials, or Generation Y, for example, as a broad generalization. This age group cut their teeth on social media. They get a bad rap sometimes because, from what I understand, they are the most educated, technically sophisticated generation ever. Yet, with their savvy in social media, often posting personal information, pictures, and opinions, we have to be careful that we don't misunderstand that Millennials—or anyone for that matter with frequent social media use—might not prefer public recognition."

"Privacy can be complex; I could see that."

"Right, just because you may post an opinion or a picture of your grilled cheese sandwich publicly on social media, doesn't mean at the office you necessarily wish for recognition in a public format, in front of anyone at any time. Although, I did read that most Millennials like to have their recognition shared in some way, so others see they've been recognized. But proceeding with caution is so important and generalizing an entire group is often unhelpful to everyone."

"That goes for anyone, which is why each person should be treated individually when it comes to recognition. That no one-size-fits-all thing we've been talking about."

Mark continued, "Yet . . . the same article said that more than any other segment of the U.S. population, Millennials are accustomed to feedback, rewards, and recognition and therefore have higher expectations than others especially in the form of recognition and even meaningful rewards. And still, it's important not to generalize or assume. Be aware of your audience and adjust because the bottom line is that it's still personal to each individual. Each person needs to feel authentically recognized."

"Those are good points; it could be easy to make assumptions." David added, "I get the feeling something else is bugging you about this."

"True, and it's one I've been thinking about for a while, and it's a biggie. But look at the time. I will leave you in suspense and see if you can guess it when we get back together."

David told Mark that he would humor him with the guessing and their 20 minutes were up. They planned to check their calendars in the next few days to set up their next meeting.

Fundamental 1: Rewards Are Not the Same as Recognition

After two weeks, Mark and David met for coffee in the cafeteria. Mark began, "So, have you guessed what's bugging me?"

"I have a short attention span," said David. "Refresh my memory."

Ignoring the sarcasm, Mark said, "What's bugging me is rewards and their place in recognition. Earlier we talked about rewards doing all the talking or being front-loaded. Well, the Sebastian celebration was all about getting an award. Not a lot of substance. I think the reason that happens, and what has been bugging me, is that recognition and rewards are often viewed as the same thing, or interchangeable."

David thought for a moment and said, "We are on to a key point that is notebook worthy."

"Good! *I declare for all of humanity . . .*" Mark turned back to the Recognition Fundamentals page and wrote the first Fundamental in the notebook.

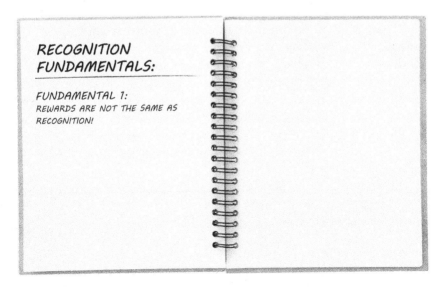

RECOGNITION FUNDAMENTALS:

FUNDAMENTAL 1:
REWARDS ARE NOT THE SAME AS RECOGNITION!

Shaking his head, David grinned and commented, "I agree. Rewards and recognition do get interchanged a lot. In fact, I'm not sure I ever separated them."

Mark nodded while David gave an example from Operations the previous year. He said that three of his team members witnessed a peer in another department receive a surprise envelope on her desk filled with $200 worth of gift cards to Bensi Corp retail, with a note from her manager, "For a job well done on the project."

Mark immediately jumped in, "Well-intentioned, and who wouldn't want gift cards, but it reeks of check-the-box for the manager. Plus the reward was in place of a real conversation. *Missed opportunity!*" Mark emphatically stated. On a roll, he brought up the point that the team members who witnessed this would be wondering when they might get their $200 worth of gift cards.

Defending the manager, David added, "Right, but I'll bet that manager didn't give it a thought beyond the rewards, like most of us have been doing, especially since there is no real acknowledgment or training for us managers in how to deliver recognition effectively." David further said that this case was tricky because, without specifics, it appeared that the reward was for *completing* a project not necessarily how well it was performed. "And," he continued, "witnesses had differing opinions on the success of the project, to begin with, so expectations for the reward, in this case, were misplaced and probably confusing. Not to mention creating unrealistic expectations for the future."

"I can picture an immediate drop in motivation, and unfortunately that may ring true for too many recognition situations." Mark reiterated David's point of all managers expecting to be intuitively effective despite not having been taught how to deliver effective recognition. "If you're not thoughtful about it, delivering recognition can be so demotivating. So, if recognition and rewards should not be interchangeable, then they should each be viewed separately. Instead, it's as though rewards become the main thing and recognition is just icing on the cake."

"I hear you. Hold that thought and hand me your markers. I just pictured something tasty yet dysfunctional," David said. He flipped a notebook page and drew the following.

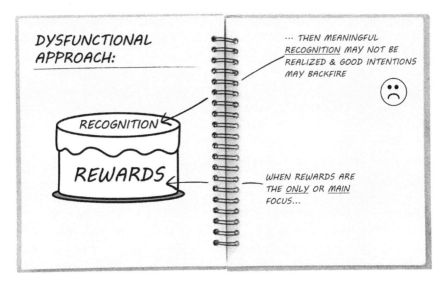

"That's it! The current general model is that rewards are the foundation to recognition, or the cake as you say. And when that is the case, authentic recognition may or may not be included or is a small part of the process. Delivering authentic recognition should not just be icing on the cake. It should come *first*, and then rewards, *if given at all*, should serve the purpose of strengthening the recognition for performance."

Jumping to his next thought, David asked Mark, "Have you ever used Bensi Corp's recognition program? At first glance, it seems typical of other companies who have them."

"I think so. I've used it a couple of times, but its main focus is on the rewards, where the recognition part is minimized. The only guidance for the program is related to the online process, which confirms the recognition training gap for managers."

"I think you're right; it's similar to other programs. I don't want our conversations to cause trouble, though, if we already have a recognition program in place," David cautioned.

"Since when!? Look, I am trying to simplify and be more effective. We know there is a better way. I am not about to take a big ol' swipe at our institution-sanctioned recognition program. I just want to spread the word on better ways of recognizing. But first we need to make sure we truly understand what we are potentially planning to implement."

"You are really fired up about this Mr. Grassroots!" David validated Mark's approach and admitted that he doesn't like to wait around either, especially when their thoughts are starting to come together.

"It's not like I'm twiddling my thumbs in Hardlines, and in the long term, I know this will help me, and I find it interesting, so yeah, I'm motivated."

David wondered, "So, what are we going to do with this information? Self-development? Or do you have grander schemes?"

Getting these thoughts down was motivating for Mark. His goal was to influence others in some way, the way his very first manager influenced him. He commented that she was very good at recognizing the value of Mark's work. He wasn't sure if she was just a natural or if someone modeled it for her, but he was grateful for the lasting benefit.

"I can see how one person can make such a difference. Think about what you do with your own team by having that modeled for you," said David.

"Good of you to notice. I have been upping my recognition game lately. We can influence others just by modeling, or even teaching."

Considering what to do with the information, David thought that it's probably not a rollout, or new program—no selling, no forms to fill out, no announcement. It would just be a new way of being. "Just some tools to help other managers."

That was exactly what Mark was thinking. Mark and David agreed that the last thing they wanted to happen was for managers to feel as though authentic recognition is another item on their to-do list. Mark even wondered if their version of recognition might complement Bensi Corp's existing recognition program.

"I told Donna we were going to develop and deliver a Lunch and Learn, starting with the managers in our division," stated

Mark. "She is intrigued and wants to see if we might even measure its impact on company performance. Love it!"

"I think you've just committed us." After a few moments, knowing Mark has worked longer with Sebastian than David has, he asked, "So what do you think Sebastian will think?"

Unsure what Sebastian would think, Mark concluded that it was okay either way for now. "Starting small and showing some value can work. Sebastian's concern is results—productivity and bottom line. I'd like to believe that Sebastian sees the investment in employees as a direct impact on the bottom line. Either way, I think we should just move forward. Besides, Donna has our backs."

"So, starting small, not worrying about buy-in or permission from other senior executives sounds great and realistic. Ideal, actually!" David did acknowledge to himself that he may need to talk up the Lunch and Learn directly with Sebastian. He didn't want to rely on Stephen's version, if Stephen shared it with Sebastian; who knows what Stephen would spin up for his own boss!

"We don't need to take on the world. In fact, we don't need to 'transform the organization.' Just think globally, act locally. Create the desired culture *around* you. Save a few lives. You get the picture."

"Honestly, saving a few lives sounds so much more doable than transforming an organization," David confessed.

They continued their conversation, and both agreed that if transforming an entire organization happened and a recognition culture emerged, then that would be incredible. "Grassroots feels authentic to me and doable for anyone. One thing we can both feel certain of, is that recognition could transform our teams," said Mark.

"Talking about these concepts have been a big help to me in understanding recognition."

"You and me both." Standing up and putting his notebook, markers, pen, and phone in his backpack, Mark concluded, "I really want to get to the nuts and bolts and continue to define recognition and discuss the *how* part of delivering it."

"We really made some progress." David added another Key Take-Away to the notebook.

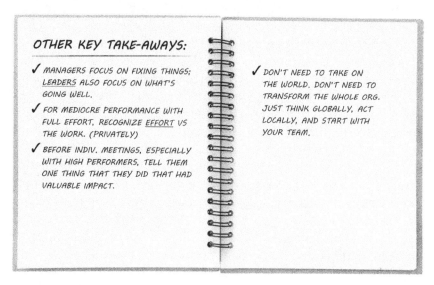

OTHER KEY TAKE-AWAYS:

✓ MANAGERS FOCUS ON FIXING THINGS; LEADERS ALSO FOCUS ON WHAT'S GOING WELL.

✓ FOR MEDIOCRE PERFORMANCE WITH FULL EFFORT, RECOGNIZE EFFORT VS THE WORK. (PRIVATELY)

✓ BEFORE INDIV. MEETINGS, ESPECIALLY WITH HIGH PERFORMERS, TELL THEM ONE THING THAT THEY DID THAT HAD VALUABLE IMPACT.

✓ DON'T NEED TO TAKE ON THE WORLD. DON'T NEED TO TRANSFORM THE WHOLE ORG. JUST THINK GLOBALLY, ACT LOCALLY, AND START WITH YOUR TEAM.

Having captured their thoughts in the notebook, they decided to set up their next meeting.

First Recognize, Then Reward (Sometimes)

Mark had several reports to develop for Hardlines this month and was doing double duty working through the process with Laura until she got up to speed in her senior buyer role. They all had work to do to be ready for month-end. David was in the same boat, and he wanted to get his six-month report in for Softlines. They decided to forgo their meeting and messaged each other since it was still on their minds.

> DAVID: While sparing me any childhood issues, why do you feel so strongly about rewards and recognition not being interchangeable? I see the missed opportunity, but what else—why do you get so fired up? Or is that enough?

MARK: I am going to respond as though you did not bring up childhood issues.

Now then, rewards and why I feel so strongly. I think mostly because while intentions are good, rewards can be the lazy way.

But I like movie tickets and gift cards.

Who doesn't? I'm not turning any gifts away. But I have noticed that rewards are often used as a motivator. And that is not always effective or sustainable compared with other meaningful ways to recognize performance.

Like pouring on gifts with the no-love thing. Almost as though the reward is distracting.

Plus, if you only give rewards, or too many, then you could create an environment where people might feel guilty if they want to bring up honest feedback about the company. Almost like buying their loyalty. And maybe we can all be bought to some degree, for some period of time, but it doesn't last, and it's certainly not interchangeable with recognizing someone.

I could totally see that. Actually, one of my earlier jobs, the GM would occasionally walk around with cool rewards for all of us like cash, tickets to Twins game. Loved it. Had no idea why we got them though. Once he laid a $50 bill on our desks—which of course we loved.

It did make it harder to voice concerns about the company. Felt guilty/ungrateful.

Bet it was fun while it lasted.

And not the only reason, but you will notice I am here and not there.

When I bring up recognition to other managers (yes, I do) I hear stuff like: "I don't have a recognition budget." More evidence recognition and rewards are treated interchangeably.

Budget. It's a first thought for sure.

I want to get the word out that it doesn't have to cost money to tell a team member that you noticed impactful performance.

So, what if there was no $$ for recognition and managers were strongly encouraged to recognize their teams without $$?

I would LOVE that. That would be a great way to simplify and help managers really think about recognition at its core. Rewards are awesome, but they have their place. More effective if it's the LAST thought, not the FIRST as we have been preaching at one another.

Icing on the cake... so flipping the model upside down.

Okay I'm going to sketch our new cake...gimme a few. I'm sure you have reports to review or write or something...

Also, seems it would have been more efficient to actually meet instead.

Agree, but we were on a roll.

Mark got out the notebook and quickly drew a cake similar to what David created earlier. He took a photo of it and sent it to David. When David opened the message and enlarged the image on his screen, he saw the following.

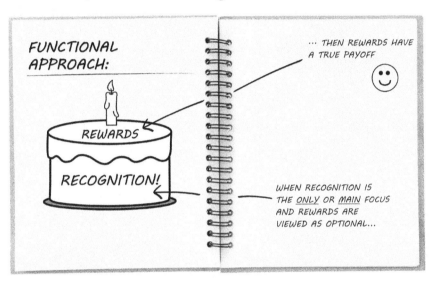

DAVID: That looks familiar sorta. Way to put the "fun" in functional.

MARK: I try. How do YOU read this?

Opposite of our first cake. Focus on delivering authentic recognition FIRST that MAY include rewards...

Which would be only icing on the cake.

Well said.

Imagine if this were the way it was always done.

Can we just pause for a moment and imagine how that would hit loyalty for your high performers and bottom line?

This feels like progress.

Also, we talk about recognition. Making it authentic. What do we mean by that? We should clarify.

Let's. I have to think about it. I'm going to add another take-away to the notebook though, first.

OTHER KEY TAKE-AWAYS:

✓ MANAGERS FOCUS ON FIXING THINGS; LEADERS ALSO FOCUS ON WHAT'S GOING WELL.

✓ FOR MEDIOCRE PERFORMANCE WITH FULL EFFORT, RECOGNIZE EFFORT VS THE WORK. (PRIVATELY)

✓ BEFORE INDIV. MEETINGS, ESPECIALLY WITH HIGH PERFORMERS, TELL THEM ONE THING THAT THEY DID THAT HAD VALUABLE IMPACT.

✓ DON'T NEED TO TAKE ON THE WORLD. DON'T NEED TO TRANSFORM THE WHOLE ORG. JUST THINK GLOBALLY, ACT LOCALLY, AND START WITH YOUR TEAM.

✓ $$ NOT REQUIRED TO RECOGNIZE.

How to Deliver Authentic Recognition

Recognition Delivery Essentials (TIPSS)

MARK: Know what I respect about Donna?

DAVID: Narrow it down.

She wants to do the right thing and loves to learn.

Also, my own boss asked me for my opinion. Pinch me.

Now the truth comes out.

Seriously. It's the beginnings of recognition. It makes me feel incredibly valued that she acknowledged my manager survey ratings and wanted to know why I score higher in the valued/appreciated category.

Cool. Did you update her on how far we've gotten?

Went through notebook. She's intrigued and said it made sense to her. Wants to find ways to help us and our teams feel more valued. She liked the simplicity.

She knows what she could have done differently with Ajay, but is unclear how.

I am sure we can help with that once we get there. BTW, I already have her kicking off the lunch and learn.

Me too, or some involvement. Told her I'd give her periodic updates when we meet.

You for sure have now committed us.

That train has left the station.

In this case, I'm good with continuing the conversation. I'm seeing that this is something I can actually do and make a difference with my team. And me too.

Small effort

...for big payoff. My favorite formula.

So, what's next? Where'd we leave off?

Delivery. The thing Donna is asking about. The HOW to deliver recognition so there is payoff. Crass way to put it.

We would word it differently, but I like the idea of being open about motivation. Everyone wants same thing. Takes suspicion out.

Are people that damaged at work? Say something nice, they get suspicious?

It's an org culture thing, plus some individual baggage. Last year in Ops, I sent an email complimenting the work of my employee. Haven't done that much and the person thought I had an agenda. Like I was priming him for something I wanted later.

Could see how people go there and think it's conditional if they're not used to recognition. Consistency helps. Think globally, act locally and we change culture a little at a time if I may repeat myself.

Global/local—my favorite approach. So, back to "HOW" we deliver recognition.

Lunch tomorrow?

Salad time again. I'll be thinking about how to deliver.

I can make that work–if we're not that productive tho, then let's cut it short and use another time to shoot the breeze.

Agree. See ya then.

After sitting down with their lunches, Mark and David compared their thinking on how to deliver recognition.

"Recognition payoff comes down to making it authentic," said David.

"And that comes down to how it is communicated to the employee. Yet, the lack of training or mentoring, except for the lucky few, is a barrier that prevents the communication portion of recognition from being effective to our team members."

"Every manager could take a quiz and, if asked, they would answer yes, it is important to recognize team members. So, we know the right answer; we just don't do it."

"I feel strongly that making it easy for managers is important. It should be simple enough to not feel like another to-do in their already demanding jobs," said Mark.

"Doing *both*, making it easy and using a simple approach, could make a difference. Give me simple and effective every time because my mostly 'do-nothing' approach isn't the best."

"It would be good to walk through an example of when one of us was recognized well. Think about a time when you felt so proud of the recognition you received. Maybe something you were looking forward to telling Rebecca."

David thought for a moment, and one, in particular, stood out from the best manager he had in his career. He briefly summarized, "When I worked in Operations, we were under pressure because of an IT issue that we called Severity Level 1—meaning top priority, all-hands-on-deck. A manufacturing issue had occurred in Asia, and, as usual, we had little influence. I pressed my team to do what we could in spite of it not being 'our fault' and we worked through it. The best part was that my boss told me that he really appreciated how I always—and especially this time—lead a team under pressure and specifically that I do not spend time or energy blaming or throwing my hands in the air."

"Nice!"

"There's more! My boss told me he was especially impressed that, when another leader voiced a 'who caused this' type of question, I quickly redirected the conversation to solving the problem. He said that I relentlessly—yes, he used that word—work to solve the problem even when the issue is largely outside of my influence. He credited me with the issue being resolved quickly by leading with that approach."

"Awesome! It's good to see your style get recognized so well. You do stand out as a leader who owns a problem that is not the team's fault, and you help to solve it anyway rather than walking away."

"It was really nice to have my leadership noticed."

"So, he was specific, and he talked about the impact."

"It was very sincere," David added, "and it was the very next day. And I think the reason it was so memorable was that it was also very personal to me and my work style. It felt great to hear a thank you in such a specific and sincere way. In fact, now that I think about it, a reward of some sort was not part of the way he recognized me. And still, it was so memorable. So, if done well, verbal recognition can have a longer lasting impact than a reward."

Mark nodded thoughtfully and said, "That's how it's done, folks! Let's get these down." He turned the page in the notebook, and they listed what they called Essentials (the *how*) for authentic recognition delivery.

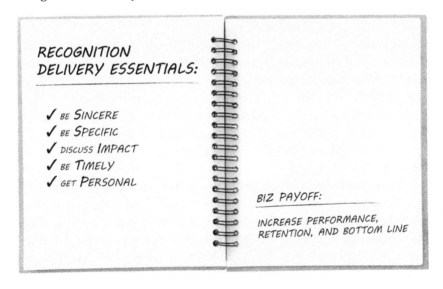

RECOGNITION
DELIVERY ESSENTIALS:

✓ BE SINCERE
✓ BE SPECIFIC
✓ DISCUSS IMPACT
✓ BE TIMELY
✓ GET PERSONAL

BIZ PAYOFF:

INCREASE PERFORMANCE, RETENTION, AND BOTTOM LINE

Now that they had decided on the Recognition Delivery Essentials, it was important to include the business payoff for recognizing performance (the *why*). They knew they could draw from their earlier research and discussions to clarify what that business payoff is.

They both liked the idea of keeping these two ideas on one page. So, in addition to performance recognition, making everyone feel great, which goes a long way at work (and a good attitude is certainly helpful), Mark translated the research into what he called the Biz Payoff reminder and added that in business terms at the bottom of the notebook.

"These Essentials seem to capture the heart of delivering recognition. And I so appreciate the simplicity," said David.

"Now that I see this in black and white, I am not sure I included all of these when I recognized a team member recently. In fact, I'm thinking about when I recognized my analyst earlier. If I had thought about it a little more deliberately, I could have told her more about the *impact* her work had. I am sure that would have been great for her to hear. Imagine the payoff when all the Essentials are included! Sometimes with just one minute of thought, literally."

David validated that it doesn't take much time and just a little energy—the good kind of energy.

"I think my approach has been to thank the person for what they've done specifically calling out their personal contribution to the team's success. I didn't separate the individual from the team and make it very personal. But I can see that the more of these Essentials we include, the bigger the payoff. It especially makes sense when I think about the example from my former boss."

"The order really isn't important, but include all when possible."

They reiterated from a previous conversation that the criteria for recognizing someone be that the work had valuable impact. They believed that managers could make this part of regular conversations more often and during individual meetings with their team. They played this out to determine whether it was realistic using smaller, everyday examples.

"Let's say a team member shared a great business book with my manager—or someone else—who loved it and couldn't stop talking about it. And let's say my manager hears about it," Mark continued. "It would be simple the next time you run into your employee to say, 'Hey, there's some good buzz about the book you recommended to so-and-so. I hear she loves it.'"

"Good enough, right?" Mark asked. "It passes *Sincere*, *Timely*, *Personal*, and *Specific*. What about *Impact*, though? It had an impact, but we don't know what it is except she's talking about it and she loved it."

"The bottom line is that it will add to the person's day, and yours too, just for deciding to be generous with that small recognition. These kinds of things begin to add up for employees; you can at least see how you can reduce the risk of regrettable turnover. And why not target your high performers? Sometimes you even know there was an impact, but you don't know to what level," said David.

"I feel an acronym coming on!"

"If it helps me remember better, I'm all ears."

Mark did some rearranging of the steps and rewrote the following on the next pages, remembering to include the business payoff at the bottom.

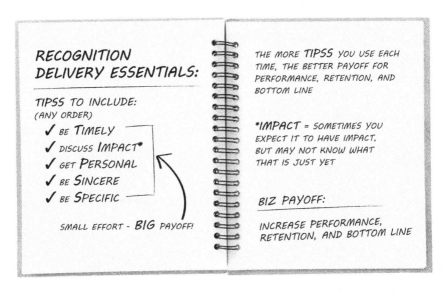

RECOGNITION DELIVERY ESSENTIALS:

TIPSS TO INCLUDE:
(ANY ORDER)
✔ BE TIMELY
✔ DISCUSS IMPACT*
✔ GET PERSONAL
✔ BE SINCERE
✔ BE SPECIFIC

SMALL EFFORT - BIG PAYOFF!

THE MORE TIPSS YOU USE EACH TIME, THE BETTER PAYOFF FOR PERFORMANCE, RETENTION, AND BOTTOM LINE

*IMPACT = SOMETIMES YOU EXPECT IT TO HAVE IMPACT, BUT MAY NOT KNOW WHAT THAT IS JUST YET

BIZ PAYOFF:

INCREASE PERFORMANCE, RETENTION, AND BOTTOM LINE

"Nice! I can remember this! As in, 'Let me give you some TIPSS.' It uncomplicates it, and the order doesn't matter. Got it!" David said.

"Good, because I am kinda proud of it," Mark replied. "Let's test them out; I think I skipped the *Impact* part when I recognized my analyst recently." Before David could respond, Mark added, "You be my analyst, and I'll be me. We'll do a reenactment."

After joking around about it and acknowledging that role-playing can be awkward, Mark began the practice by knocking lightly on the lunch table.

"Good morning, Rita. Glad I caught up with you first thing because I want to compliment you on the job well done last week."

Acting as Rita, David perked up and looked slightly awkward.

Earnestly practicing, Mark continued, "I don't mean to embarrass you, but it's important that you know how impressive it was the way you met our deadline with such competence and grace. With Ajay leaving and Donna pushing the accelerator, your portion of the Manhattan prototype stores analysis gave Donna a big boost to have something very positive at a time when Hardlines really needed it. And, adding the Q&A for anticipated analysis for her was outstanding and saved her some heavy lifting from doing it herself. In fact, your third question was the first thing the CEO asked. Having the numbers ready was so helpful. Thank you for doing that so well last week and for delivering more than was required of you. It made a big difference to Donna and to me, personally."

Breaking character, David responded, "Wow, you said a lot, but it seemed to flow pretty well. I could see feeling slightly awkward receiving such a specific and personal recognition, but mostly it made me feel appreciated and proud. I was wondering though, as Rita, if I might hear from Donna since she was so pleased."

"Good point," said Mark. "I will see about Donna circling back to Rita too."

"But it does bring up the point not to hold back, or rely on others to recognize someone if we know we can also give some praise."

"Yes, Donna may or may not get back to Rita, and I certainly don't want to set expectations that she will, just in case."

David added, "Right, you'd be setting up both Donna and Rita."

"As for being awkward, I think that's important to acknowledge. Everyone dreads the awkward. The manager may dread an awkward conversation, but the employee would feel more awkward in the moment, with no time to mentally prepare. Don't let that stop you. The goal is that people should know their work is valued even if someone feels awkward. Plus I think it gets *way* easier for everyone when recognition conversations happen more regularly."

"As for the flow," Mark continued, "I ran through the TIPSS in my head. It took only a minute at most for me to think of the main points for each. The *Timely* part is a freebie if you are actually, well, timely. I especially wanted to focus on what *Specific* thing she did and the *Impact*. I recognized Rita last week, but it was a little more generic, and I think she felt appreciated, but I can imagine when I get very specific like I did with the Q&A and tell her how it impacted Donna, as an executive, that would really seal *Personal* and *Sincere*."

"So, once you say what *Specific* thing someone did and the *Impact* it had, there is little room for questioning whether the recognition is *Personal* and *Sincere*," David summarized. "So, taking the Severity Level example I shared, my boss, whether intentional or not, told me specifically what I did and the impact I had—issues got resolved quickly. I think that may have something to do with why I remember that moment of recognition so clearly."

"He made it very memorable by being specific and telling you the impact," Mark agreed. "That probably made it feel really *Sincere* and *Personal*."

"So maybe we don't have to work so hard at *Sincere* and *Personal* if we have the other TIPSS. And as for the *Personal* component, we would need to clarify that this is not the time to border on creepy or inappropriate; *Personal* will naturally occur when you speak to the *Specifics* and *Impact*. It was sincere and personal as is. Creepy or inappropriate might be adding nonbusiness insight such as, 'So all that extra work was probably difficult with your divorce and all.' Or 'Is there something in your personal life that has inspired you to work extra hard this time?' You get the picture."

"Keep it to business impact and business motivation. Be *Sincere*, and *Personal* will come through," said David.

"Yes!"

"I would think the *Personal* and *Sincere* can happen based on the approach you take. For example, is the recognition with ten other people all at once, or is it more personal to each person and their preferences?" David asked.

"Exactly! As we talk about recognizing, we will also need to be aware, as managers, that we might be thrilled with work done well, but the employee maybe did something *else* twice as impactful that week that you didn't know about yet. So, I guess I'm saying it's important that you build the trust in these conversations and that both of you realize that it's a snapshot in time. It could be disheartening if your manager misses the big thing that week in favor of something smaller, but in the course of the conversation, you are hopefully learning more about the work that went on that week, or month. Just a caution that it can happen where you don't quite hit the target!"

"Good thought. I could see these TIPSS as a useful tool for managers in our Lunch and Learn."

"Me too. And I admit, I need some practice too. Maybe offering this to other managers would help me improve my own recognition skills. We could include practice sessions, even if it is awkward and they joke around. In fact, even better! The idea is to get more comfortable using the concepts, and why not have some fun too?"

"And, with a Lunch and Learn approach, at least at first, it doesn't really require reining in the whole executive team for support as you might need to for other training."

They both committed to practicing the TIPSS and agreed these would be a key part of their eventual Lunch and Learn. Jotting down another Key Take-Away, they parted ways.

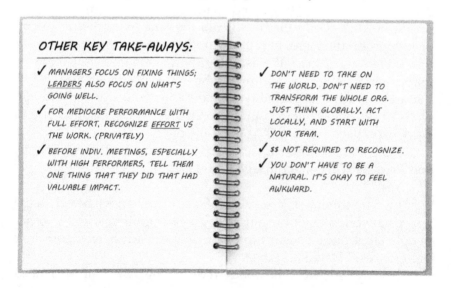

OTHER KEY TAKE-AWAYS:

✓ MANAGERS FOCUS ON FIXING THINGS; LEADERS ALSO FOCUS ON WHAT'S GOING WELL.

✓ FOR MEDIOCRE PERFORMANCE WITH FULL EFFORT, RECOGNIZE EFFORT VS THE WORK. (PRIVATELY)

✓ BEFORE INDIV. MEETINGS, ESPECIALLY WITH HIGH PERFORMERS, TELL THEM ONE THING THAT THEY DID THAT HAD VALUABLE IMPACT.

✓ DON'T NEED TO TAKE ON THE WORLD. DON'T NEED TO TRANSFORM THE WHOLE ORG. JUST THINK GLOBALLY, ACT LOCALLY, AND START WITH YOUR TEAM.

✓ $$ NOT REQUIRED TO RECOGNIZE.

✓ YOU DON'T HAVE TO BE A NATURAL. IT'S OKAY TO FEEL AWKWARD.

Fundamental 2: *How* You Deliver Is More Important Than *What* You Deliver

On the way back to his desk, Mark thought about their quick practice session. He also wondered about the big team meetings and the concepts he and David have been talking about that could have made those meetings more authentic. *How* a manager recognizes someone is fundamental; it's more important than *what* may be given as a reward. If the Delivery Essentials (TIPSS) are absent, then a reward, if given, is shallow with little payoff to performance or loyalty. As soon as he reached his office, he flipped back to the Recognition Fundamentals page and jotted down the second Fundamental. He was certain David would agree with this one.

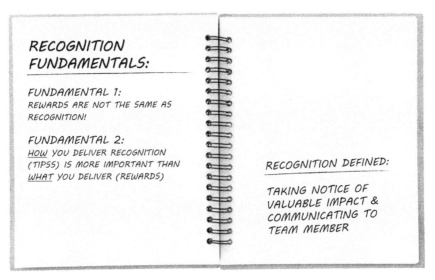

Taking a photo of the second Fundamental and sending it to David, Mark checked in to see what he thought.

> DAVID: The 2nd Fundamental is soooo true. I wonder how many people are still feeling valued or excited that they got a gift card. Did the organization get payoff from that?

MARK: Good questions.

So, let's say I get $200 reward. I'm thinking I've done something pretty important.

Well, yeah, but think back to your envelope with Bensi gift cards reward example. It's great to get, it sent an important message that it was a big deal...

Right – so imagine my $200 reward including really specific feedback on my impact from my manager. My head would spin.

Exactly. All the more reason to share the TIPSS with other managers.

Let's keep this topic going—it helps me be more aware of value/impact my team has—and how I can make a difference with them.

I'm in.

Fundamental 3: Doing *Nothing* Is Sometimes Better Than Doing *Something*

DAVID: Ready?

MARK: Cafeteria?

Sounds good – need to eat more salads and not just the bread part.

Ha! Good to know you're trainable.

Rebecca might disagree. Told me this weekend that I eat like an eight-year-old.

Um...

Never mind. See ya in 5.

Ok

David and Mark met in the cafeteria, got their salads, and found a table in the corner. David picked up on an earlier thought that they had saved for later. "So, if recognition is largely for high performers, what happens to poor performers? Should they get recognized? Who does not get recognized? I have many unanswered questions!"

These were good questions that were discussed at length. Mark and David concluded that top performers should be the main focus of recognition. Misleading or confusing the team by having equal recognition regardless of performance is unhelpful. "It may sound harsh, but I can't stand dumbing down great performance by recognizing work that doesn't deserve it. You've seen it, and I've seen it. It's demotivating when top performers see a poor performer get recognized," said Mark.

"And confusing! Why did she *also* get the shout-out when she coasted, or that guy was a jerk throughout the whole project, but he was rewarded just the same as the rest of the team?" David responded, "Most of us have witnessed something similar, and it really can create cynicism, in spite of good intentions. However, if there are small victories or areas of valuable impact for the low performers or even the jerk, then make a note and recognize that person privately. This is a judgement call but could be motivating for better performance, or with some work, even turn the person around. It depends on your intentions with this person. Is this a major HR issue? Are you managing them out for a better fit elsewhere?"

They both agreed that there could be some training in this area—do the right thing, yet don't misset expectations with someone who is not performing well.

"My first thought about handling a poor performer is similar to other ways we lead our teams—the performance is based on the situation. Of course, we always try to develop a poor performer, which is usually in everyone's best interest. However, at times, it does depend on the reason for not performing. Is this person new and can they learn? Or is this someone who is not making a valuable impact? Like any situation, the manager needs to make a decision whether to find another role, make adjustments, or manage them out."

Their discussion led to the impression that it might have on high-performing employees who are being recognized more than other employees who may not be high performers. What they knew for sure was when you treat people with integrity and equity (versus equally) the complaints are much more manageable. "It's here where the approach really matters. Are you going to parade your top performers in front of the whole team each week to recognize them, or perhaps you consider paying attention to when it should be private or public?"

David reiterated, "It's not always easy to help your employees perform at their best, but I can see how recognizing high performers is a big motivator. But is it realistic to have peak performers all the time on all of our teams? There is that bell curve," David reasoned.

"Well, we both know a large part of a manager's job is understanding the context of the skill set. Specifically, skills that may be required along with varying levels of experience for each employee mean that there will naturally be different expectations for each person. For example, a senior analyst who performs very well at a senior analyst level would have high expectations within that role. Conversely, an entry-level employee who is performing well at the entry-level job would have her own set of high expectations. Both high expectations, yet different expectations for different level jobs.

Both could be strong performers even though their impact would be at different levels."

"So, performance based on expectations of the role," summarized David.

"Exactly, and the skills they contribute to those expectations. You know, the more we talk about recognition for performance, the more I want to have simple standards in place to ensure consistency and integrity."

"That would be good. We need some organization to our conversations," said David. "I think about Stephen's approach. If you were to ask him, he would say he is pouring on the recognition. If you ask me, not so much." David continued, "I haven't really been expecting it and would rather he acknowledge my work properly or not at all. Otherwise, it's embarrassing for both of us."

"Might it help Stephen if you could model behavior down the road?"

"Maybe. Stephen is Stephen. It's disappointing to feel like I have to train my boss, but it happens." David realized that he knew a little more about this topic than he thought and wondered if other managers would feel the same way. He reminded Mark that, besides his team, he had other reasons for wanting to influence Jan as his peer manager. She's been a helpful resource for him, especially the first couple of months in his new role. "Jan may be a little misunderstood due to the pure volume of work and no substantial support from Stephen. I do wonder if she stays at Bensi Corp because she's too burned out and has no energy to look elsewhere. Or maybe she is hoping Stephen moves on. I think Stephen's generic 'Hey, great job in all you do!' or some version of that is irritating her. I know his intentions are good, but he can spare me also."

"'The road to hell,' as we say," said Mark.

"Let me give you an example. Stephen tossed two sample neckties to Jan and me in the conference room as a 'thank you for all you do.' The ties were reject samples, by the way, and had runs in the fabric."

"That's rough."

"Jan was especially unenthused about the 'reward.' He suggested that the tie wasn't for her, that she could give it to her husband."

"When did Jan get married?"

"She didn't."

"Yikes! I think that approach would throw me right into the fetal position. Maybe there is no influencing him."

David reminded Mark that clients love Stephen and that outside of Softlines, people get a charge out of him and think he is pretty entertaining.

"I think I would like to start referring to everyone as simply, 'friend,' like he does; 'good to see you, friend!' His country-clubby approach is kinda enviable. He's likable, irritating, and amusing. Only he can pull that off!"

"No argument here. That three-pronged approach is nearly impressive." David admitted that he was actually glad that Stephen lets him do his thing. He further added that Stephen's version of recognition and support is not motivating or helpful and is certainly not amusing. "Honestly, he would be better off doing nothing."

"I think so, honestly."

"I wonder the same thing about peer-to-peer recognition. I admit I haven't touched that with a ten-foot pole. I suppose I have complimented my peers a time or two in the past, but it's been in private or during a conversation. Probably not very often, though," said David.

"I'd love to see the peer-to-peer approach be more private. I've experienced peer-to-peer recognition as an optional thing people can do before a meeting or in general through a recognition program. It's a little shaky, and I think it can get messy."

"Meaning?"

"Well, it's optional so some will do it and some won't. And it's always public. And well, we just had that talk about public recognition cautions. But the trickiest thing, and I don't mean to be a jerk, is that it can also be confusing. At one company I worked with, one of my peers made a terrible, careless error with the client, then handled it poorly by making excuses. In hindsight, and I'm guessing here, the leadership team was at a point of managing him out of the business. At that point, word was getting out about the handling of the error with the client. The next day we had a large team meeting, and a peer, who did not know about the error, gave glowing feedback to him about the project. Now, from that peer's perspective and limited exposure, it made sense, but to the rest of us, who saw the project sliding and then this behavior, it was unfortunate. At that point, what do you think the rest of us thought of peer-to-peer recognition?" asked Mark.

"*And* that just made that manager's job harder."

"*And* the guy who received the recognition from his peer looked really embarrassed because of the timing. I felt bad for the guy."

"Right. So we're not saying don't let people know when they do well, and maybe they especially need to hear it in times like this, but to make it public and confuse others, and then create a bad taste for recognition? I see the risk."

"I think it can be done maybe best in private, and even better, include the person's manager, so they know too."

David thought about this and decided some peer-to-peer feedback for Jan is in order. He knows he may not be perfect at it, but he will use the TIPSS as his guide. And after the brief practice he and Mark had, David was thinking more and more how much Jan would value meaningful recognition. He decided he would do this in earnest next chance he gets.

While not all ineffective examples are as extreme as Stephen's or this peer-to-peer example, they realized their third Fundamental of recognition for performance. Picking up the marker, Mark wrote it down in the notebook.

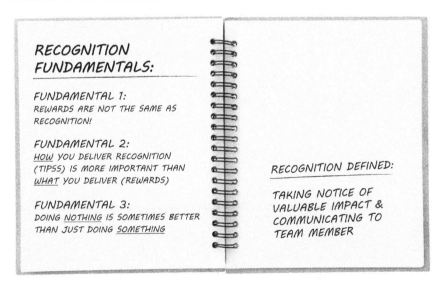

RECOGNITION FUNDAMENTALS:

FUNDAMENTAL 1:
REWARDS ARE NOT THE SAME AS RECOGNITION!

FUNDAMENTAL 2:
HOW YOU DELIVER RECOGNITION (TIPSS) IS MORE IMPORTANT THAN WHAT YOU DELIVER (REWARDS)

FUNDAMENTAL 3:
DOING NOTHING IS SOMETIMES BETTER THAN JUST DOING SOMETHING

RECOGNITION DEFINED:

TAKING NOTICE OF VALUABLE IMPACT & COMMUNICATING TO TEAM MEMBER

They finished their lunch and each headed back to their separate offices. On the way back, David started a follow-up thought and sent Mark a message.

DAVID: Honestly how many managers would offer such a lame reward like Stephen did with the ties?

MARK: Not many. But many might not be as effective as they think. Don't-know-what-you-don't-know kinda thing. I'm not gonna lie – Stephen's drama entertains up until it's at the expense of his people.

And I promise to reprimand myself for finding it entertaining.

Even tho Stephen is an extreme example, it can be true—recognizing someone ineffectively can be worse than not at all.

...

You run the risk of backfiring and demotivating. People can get cynical, etc., as we've said.

Let me know if I can jump in here anytime.

Okay, I will...

Anywaaaay,...we are all good-intentioned, and I believe there is a quote about the road to hell and what it is paved with.

Yup. So many examples of that. Makes me wonder how many times I've done it. And thanks – it's nice to jump in to the conversation.

I'll make it up to you and capture another take-away. The list is growing.

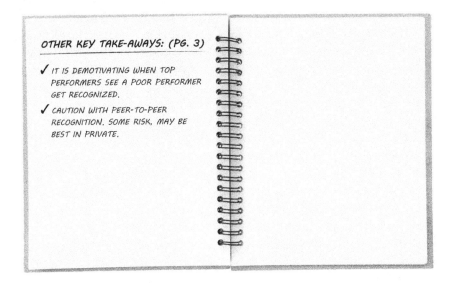

OTHER KEY TAKE-AWAYS: (PG. 3)

✓ IT IS DEMOTIVATING WHEN TOP PERFORMERS SEE A POOR PERFORMER GET RECOGNIZED.

✓ CAUTION WITH PEER-TO-PEER RECOGNITION. SOME RISK, MAY BE BEST IN PRIVATE.

Donna and Mark's Mutual Admiration

"I know I've thanked you before, but I do appreciate your talking me off the ledge during the Ajay announcement. It was good to hear the things I'm doing right," Donna confided to Mark.

They met for their monthly status meeting, and Mark readily admitted, "All true. I am your number one fan. You have championed my career and supported me unconditionally, so it goes both ways!"

Donna shared with Mark that she can't help but wonder if she could have prevented Ajay from leaving—or reduced the risk of his leaving or even affected the timing—especially after some of her research on recognition. Mark told her it was possible. He also validated that she is taking it hard, and he too misses Ajay's excellent work but is confident that Laura can get up to speed. And it is important to consider that we don't always have a say when someone resigns, but, as she said, reducing the risk of regrettable turnover, or the timing of it, may be within our influence.

Donna felt the same and said she wants to learn from this. She wants to believe she has some influence over the loyalty of high performers. She mentioned the employee survey, specifically in the area of feeling appreciated. She shared that HR reported that a small percentage of managers had used the recognition program but not regularly. She said that she believes recognition is a key area for influencing loyalty and performance. Donna explained that she was thinking of using the program but then realized Mark used it a few times when it first came out in his previous role, but now he doesn't use it at all. Yet his scores are high, his turnover low, and his people highly productive.

"It's not a bad place to start," Mark said supportively. "I found it a little limiting and tied mostly to rewards with a few downsides. I do what feels easier for me. I may still tap into it for rewards occasionally, though I'm not sure. I'm still thinking that through. I do believe what David and I are pursuing with recognition, compliments our program."

"I'd love to hear more."

Mark reflected back to Donna the quarterly department meeting led by Sebastian. "I don't mean to sound ungrateful for the gift card. Truly it's great, but . . ." and explained some more of what he and David discussed. He especially emphasized, "Recognition is different from rewards; that opportunity is lost in the delivery. Finally, at least three people in Hardlines didn't pull their weight, yet they all received the same thing."

"That never sits right with me either, but I always chalked it up to reality. So, you would say find another way to show appreciation?"

Mark agreed, and before he could continue, Donna confided, "Honestly, I didn't give it much thought. I just thought that recognition was covered each year in the annual performance review and during the annual meeting."

"It can be, and it's great, but we as managers can do more in our day-to-day to help people feel their work is valued. That goes a long way in motivation."

"I hardly ever did that for Ajay. I am not saying it's *the* reason he left. What bothers me is I believe if I would have noticed and recognized the value he brought, I may have been trusted to have that career conversation on a much deeper level and possibly influenced the timing."

"Possibly. One of the issues is that, as managers, we are inherently expected to be naturals and good at something that can have such an impact. There is a real training gap for managers in recognition. And it's something David and I are looking into further with our Lunch and Learn."

"Have you been trained? You're good at delivering recognition. Your team is strong, loyal, productive, happy . . ."

"Thanks for recognizing the impact of my work, Donna!" They both laughed. "I have never had training in how to recognize someone. I am seeing that there is more I can do, and I have some gaps that came through in my employee survey results, in spite of what you think. However, I did have a manager who modeled recognition well for me in the past. The main difference it made for me was to understand from the team member perspective how important it is. I am thoughtful with my delivery, yet I still feel like I am cobbling it together. It is one of the reasons David and I saw the need to formalize thoughts on recognition and how it can be done. *And*, why not train managers, for goodness sakes!"

Laughing was an effortless part of their relationship.

"So, do you feel that I value your work and the impact you have?"

"I do feel valued. Recognition comes in many forms, and 18 months in this role I am experiencing them. When you ask for my advice and even take it sometimes, that is recognizing my skills. The nature of our relationship—your mentoring me—tells me you have confidence in my doing a great job."

"It seems like I am only providing partial recognition."

"There is room for every manager to be more explicit in letting their people know their work is valued. That is what we intend to talk about in our Lunch and Learn. We have everything to gain when we can deliver recognition more clearly and more often. I get a big rush from seeing that my team feels valued for their work, but I am learning that I can improve to make my approach more impactful."

"To be clear Mark, your work is impactful and valuable. For example, I am so grateful for you mentoring Laura, sticking with her through our work cycle to ensure she can be successful. It helped her, the team, and me personally. I was completely at ease knowing you had this, and I could focus on other areas. Thank you for that!"

"Thank you, Donna! It was my pleasure to help out."

"I can see that I can do more to help my team feel more valued in less generic ways. It hasn't always come naturally for me. I would love to support the training and learn from it. I can see that I've been doing very little to recognize the team."

"Well your support is wonderful, and we will all benefit!" Mark agreed.

Donna asked Mark to bring her up to speed with the rest of the conversations he and David were exploring. She wants to support this and even participate, especially since this is a growth area for her.

Mark picked up where he and Donna left off previously when he shared the notebook with her. He emphasized the goal again, of delivering a Lunch and Learn, reminding her that it will include plenty of science behind organizational payoff for recognition.

"That would especially appeal to some leaders as you know—the case for *why* recognition is important in organizations."

"It's important!"

"I don't foresee major roadblocks, but if you run into obstacles with senior leaders or anyone undermining what you are doing, let me know how I can help. This is too valuable."

"I am never surprised by your support and credibility to make things move. I so appreciate it."

"My pleasure. I love the vision for this." This discussion—learning new concepts that help increase performance, the conversation, the vision—all of it was energizing to Donna, and more and more she could see herself implementing these concepts personally, especially the TIPSS. It is so helpful to have a plan!

They spent the last 15 minutes covering their monthly meeting, skipping over a few routine things. As Mark folded his laptop, they both agreed that this was time well spent.

Walking back to his office, Mark was thinking how helpful it was to talk through more of the recognition concepts with Donna and how her research has helped confirm the ideas that he and David had been working on. Her support was very reassuring. Mark began walking a little faster. He couldn't wait to fill David in.

Recognition Delivery Approaches

David stopped by Jan's office, "Knock, knock."

"Oh, hi David. What brings you here?"

"Well Jan, I'm thinking it's high time I let you know how much I appreciate your help as I figure out my role here."

"Okaaaay?"

"That is why I stopped by."

Jan was taken off guard a little but replied, "Okay."

"I don't mean to embarrass you or anything. I just want you to know that I could not have done this without your support. That first month, you helped me navigate month-end, so I could look like I knew what I was doing. You also helped me save time the next month when you told me to scrap the analyst section that was going to be obsolete. I know I thanked you at the time, but I want you to know how valuable that was to me. It helped me look sharper than I felt at the time, and it saved me a weekend, plus one evening. And I'm sure my family thanks you too. So thank you, Jan. I enjoy collaborating with you and please know I'm here to support you too."

"I don't know what to say. Thank you for saying that. I know you appreciated it. It's nice of you to let me know that it mattered so much to you."

David was transparent with Jan about recognition. He let her know that he intends to do this more with his team especially after the recognition information he and Mark have been talking about. That reminded Jan of a recent Stephen story, and she shared it with David. After a while, they both laughed about it, and she gave David permission to share it with Mark later.

That afternoon, Mark and David met again. Recognition delivery approaches were on David's mind. Especially since his conversation with Jan.

"Okay, I'm eager to explore how to make recognition more personal to each person," said David. "Even though I may have done okay recently on that score. I recognized Jan for helping me in my role."

"Nice! How did it go?"

David relayed his approach and how great it felt for both of them. Before he shared the Stephen story Jan disclosed, he was curious about delivery methods to see if he might have tried a different approach.

"So tell me your favorite way of delivering recognition? Email, verbal, voicemail, skywriter?" asked David.

"I mix it up because there are so many approaches that can work well: in person, email, thank you note . . . "

"Voicemail, in private, in public," added David. "While we are at it, let's flush out our second Fundamental, *How* you deliver recognition is more important than *What* you deliver.' Let's write down some approaches." David opened the notebook and wrote the following.

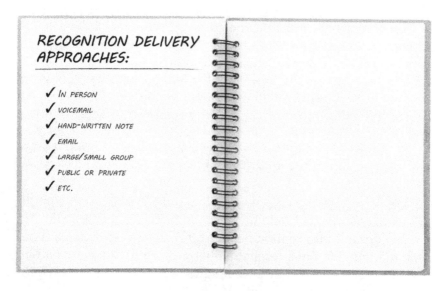

RECOGNITION DELIVERY APPROACHES:

✓ IN PERSON
✓ VOICEMAIL
✓ HAND-WRITTEN NOTE
✓ EMAIL
✓ LARGE/SMALL GROUP
✓ PUBLIC OR PRIVATE
✓ ETC.

"So, how do you decide?" David asked.

"Well, first of all, call me crazy, but honestly I ask my team members how they want to be recognized."

David chortled and said, "That's brilliant. Seriously, why not? So obvious."

"Recognition does not have to be a big fat secret. Some transparency in recognition would be refreshing."

"Agree. I was transparent with Jan on my recognizing my teams more. It felt right to say that. So, how do your team members respond to being asked?"

"Well, I started the new year during my bi-weekly meetings with each team member to talk about goals and objectives as usual. I was having a conversation with one team member about the impact of her work and said I would be sure to mention it at the department meeting. She seemed to be uncomfortable with that idea, and it occurred to me to just ask her what she'd prefer. That migrated into asking everyone. I even created a handy form for my other team members to fill out. These go in their file to make it easy to keep track and eventually revisit in case they change their minds. In my team member's case, she expressed that she would prefer an email of acknowledgment and copy the team and a few key executives. That was more personal for her. I've learned to add notes as I get to know each person, especially if I choose to include a reward. This helps me remember and makes it more personal."

"Nice! That makes sense. I'd love a copy of that handy form. It also sets them up for not being skeptical or taken off guard."

"Sure, I can share it. Let me show you what it looks like." Mark found the file and showed David how simple the document was.

Quick Tool: How Do You Wish To Be Recognized?

Don't guess. Ask your team member. Completing this form together can open up a great conversation. In addition, you as a manager will better understand your team member's preferences, enabling successful recognition. Keep this in the employee's file and check in periodically to see if preferences change. Your team member will welcome this!

Team Member's Name:

You Might Say to Your Team Member: *My intention is to reflect back to you on a more consistent basis when your work shows special value and has an impact. I want to make sure that I understand your preferences so that when I recognize your work, it can be most successful for both of us.*

Approach: Circle any of the approaches that would be okay with you.

- Face-to-face
- Voicemail
- Handwritten note
- Email just to you
- Email and copy key people
- Public recognition in front of small group or large group
- Others?

David pursued the topic, "So you learn how your team members want to be recognized. . . . Then what?"

"Well, I know for sure who does *not* like to have all attention on them, and who would prefer to be dancing on a table with laser lights pointing at them, or somewhere in between."

"You are more the table-laser-light guy, I think."

"For sure. But I do get that one person's joy is another's mortification."

"So true. So Jan shared a Stephen story about his attempt to 'motivate her,'" David air-quoted.

"This I gotta hear."

"Okay. Apparently, Stephen called Jan on her cell and said he wanted to see her as soon as possible in his office."

"Stop there. I don't care how much of a high performer you are; those are scary words."

"Exactly," David continued, "So, Jan stopped what she was doing and went to his office as summoned. Stephen apparently told her that he wanted to thank her for 'all she has done last year'—and those are Jan's air quotes, not mine—then proceeded to give her more store tie samples that just arrived on his desk. The very ones we all know were rejects by clients."

"Hard to undo that. And why was he so scary and secretive?"

That question made them both pause.

"Well, it was spontaneous and driven by the arrival of the tie package on his desk. So he probably didn't give much thought to his approach, which tends to be his M.O."

"I wonder if 'Hey, step into my office for a minute,' happens more than we think. All kinds of scary thoughts may go through an employee's mind when those words are heard from the boss," said Mark.

"Either way, maybe when that happens, the employee walks out relieved that they didn't get reprimanded, or even sacked. If I'm being charitable, I'd say that the good intentions are undeniable, but what a lost opportunity on many levels."

"More and more, I feel so fortunate that I had a boss, at one point, who modeled for me some healthy approaches with his team," mentioned Mark. "Not perfect, but usually pretty effective. A lot of people don't have that."

"Either they haven't had it modeled or have never acquired the skills along the way. All the more reason to pursue recognition concepts, spread the word, and be more deliberate about the way we deliver recognition."

Mark agreed and shared that his former boss was very transparent about recognizing him, and Mark said that it really stayed with him. "He would say something like 'Hey, Mark, come into my office. I want to recognize you for something.'"

"Didn't that take the surprise out of it?" asked David.

Mark said that he was still surprised at the content of what he was going to tell him. He also claimed that being surprised was too often overrated. "You know what I thought when he said that? 'Oh, goody goody!' Honestly, I did!"

"I could envision that, and it's fun to anticipate for a few minutes. Some surprises can scare the bejesus out of people. And there is no place for that in the workplace."

"None whatsoever. So I have to ask, does Jan just openly share these examples with you, or was it just because you were there at the right time, right place?"

David could see where Mark might be headed with the question. "Jan seems to trust me; certainly I trust her. She steered me in the right direction many times when I first took this role. She has a lot to offer, and I see some energy with her yet. So we have a trusting relationship, and yes, she shares at times, but isn't really a griper."

"I also have a good impression of Jan."

"I did share with her some of our early recognition concepts. I gotta tell you, she is very soured on recognition, but our conversation is continuing by her choice. It seems all she can see is what is *not* occurring with her boss. I hope she can see the benefits by focusing more on recognition with her team. I think she'll get there."

"If she wants authentic recognition, it will need to come from others, not her boss. And it would be awesome for her to get that endorphin rush and increase her leadership skills when she takes the time and learns to recognize her team."

"Me, too, for that matter."

"So, don't scare them! Is that what we just established?" Mark asked.

"Thumbs up!"

Mark and David weren't sure where the 'don't scare them' concern belonged but would keep it in mind as they decided to take a closer look at the approaches they wrote down. They began with voicemail.

"Rebecca leaves me voicemails to thank me for doing stuff. And that is her only purpose for the call. I dig that."

"She would do that, fabulous person that she is. Why doesn't she leave her job and come here?" asked Mark for the hundredth time. "Seriously, I know what you mean. My previous boss left me voicemails acknowledging something I contributed that week. It's really nice."

"I think Stephen's approach is fairly common. I'll get voicemails with to-dos that end with a loose form of recognition, 'Hey, we are all doing great this month . . . ' It's fine, but imagine if that 'doing great' thing was stand-alone and not mixed with an ask of some sort."

That gave them something to ponder before they moved on to handwritten notes versus email. They both liked the idea as a way to shake it up a bit, and it's a highly unexpected and under-rated approach. They imagined that some managers would use that approach and some wouldn't. What they like about email is that it's a permanent record, and you can copy others.

"I've often read to put positive things in writing. I think that's a good practice," Mark said. The subject line could be used to get attention and especially to remember not to scare the person and to be clear on intention. "No need to be mysterious."

"If I were to see 'Thank you' in a subject line? Guess which email I am opening first!" David added.

Several thoughts surfaced from their conversation. Mark interrupted the flow to make sure they got some of the ideas down. Once he did that, and with David's input, he drew an arrow next to each approach and wrote a corresponding idea to consider on the next page of the notebook. Both were satisfied with capturing their thoughts in this way.

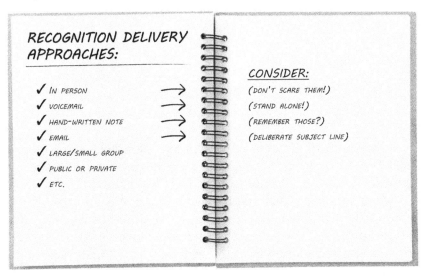

"Okay, that looks good so far. We need a couple more," Mark prompted. "What about for the large and small group approach?"

They talked about whether recognition is something the rest of the team and a senior leader should witness. What they concluded is that it's important to understand your team member's preferences.

"With a large or small group approach, it is not good to assume it's always a group thing," said Mark.

"Or a public thing. Your recognition preference form could really be handy here."

Mark added two more considerations to the large or small and the public or private approaches.

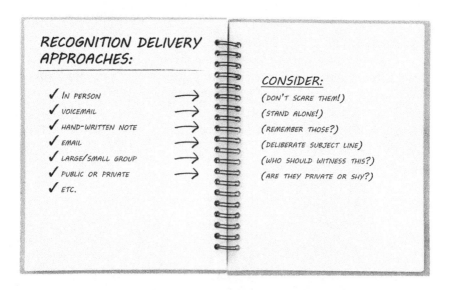

RECOGNITION DELIVERY APPROACHES:

CONSIDER:

✓ IN PERSON → (DON'T SCARE THEM!)
✓ VOICEMAIL → (STAND ALONE!)
✓ HAND-WRITTEN NOTE → (REMEMBER THOSE?)
✓ EMAIL → (DELIBERATE SUBJECT LINE)
✓ LARGE/SMALL GROUP → (WHO SHOULD WITNESS THIS?)
✓ PUBLIC OR PRIVATE → (ARE THEY PRIVATE OR SHY?)
✓ ETC.

"This is really helping me. I feel like I am getting training in this! And I've noticed that we rather fancy ourselves experts in recognition. Look at us just deciding this," David added.

More seriously, Mark said, "What we have been experts in is historically complicating or limiting recognition. I would say that we are surfacing what is relatable and what makes sense for most of us, bringing recognition for our teams back to intrinsic motivation versus extrinsic."

"Those are some five dollar words. Where are you going with that? Rewards?" David asked.

"When we talk about approaches and making it authentic, it's because we believe that recognition can be very motivating. Motivation leads to all the impactful things like performance, retention, and bottom line—all the things we've been talking about—and research has proven this. So, for motivation to be sustainable, it must come from the inside out—intrinsically."

"Versus extrinsically. When we just put rewards in front of people and not give care to the approach, at best it serves as a propping up, at worst it's demotivating."

"Well said."

"Sounds good, and before we part let me add that I know we talked about rewards not being the same as recognition. Still, we need to address rewards."

Mark glanced at his watch and agreed that they still have some key things to talk about regarding reward guidelines in terms of time, budget, and so on. He was in agreement and added, "Because rewards are appropriate and appreciated and wonderful, too."

"Those were usually the first questions I had, in the past of course!" David admitted. "What is my budget for spending on rewards? What should I get the employee?"

Mark suggested that they hold off with authentic recognition approaches until next time.

"Good summary. Let's hit that up next time. Maybe do a bit of research in between?" David suggested.

They both liked the plan, and David agreed to set up a meeting request for next time, but first, he wanted to include another Key Take-Away in the notebook.

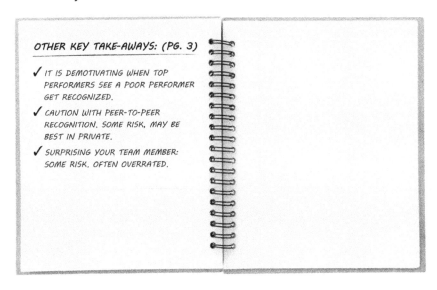

OTHER KEY TAKE-AWAYS: (PG. 3)

✓ IT IS DEMOTIVATING WHEN TOP
  PERFORMERS SEE A POOR PERFORMER
  GET RECOGNIZED.

✓ CAUTION WITH PEER-TO-PEER
  RECOGNITION. SOME RISK. MAY BE
  BEST IN PRIVATE.

✓ SURPRISING YOUR TEAM MEMBER:
  SOME RISK. OFTEN OVERRATED.

Reward Talk

DAVID: How's the reward research going?

I've done none.

MARK: Don't make me get my cape out!

I'm suddenly motivated!

Besides Donna's earlier research? I found reward guidelines that mostly focus on budget allowance. But I want to add our own thoughts to it.

Good. Let's get some standards around that. How often, how much $, etc.

There are some guidelines out there. I can show you now if you want to grab a quick coffee.

I have 30 minutes – we're not meeting until next week anyway – so let's go.

K – meet ya at Cuppa downstairs.

They met up, and Mark flipped to the page where he had captured some recognition delivery considerations earlier and showed them

to David. "These are additional guidelines I found while researching rewards," he told David.

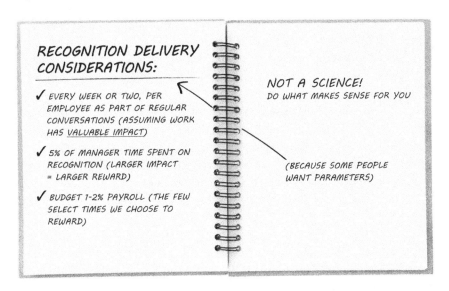

"These are just *considerations* based on some benchmarking that
I did. Every manager needs to do what makes sense."

"It's good to have some expectations for managers," David cautioned. "So if I have 12 employees, and we meet once a week, or
every two weeks, I am doing this 6 to 12 times a week? Seems like
a lot."

"It might seem like a lot. It *is* a lot of time when we go with the
common traditional approach of rewards first and *maybe* authentic
recognition. It's not a lot of time when we simplify it as we have
been suggesting. We usually meet with our employees anyway;
build your recognition conversation in then! Don't make it a big
production. When the value and impact are viewed more broadly,
such as the examples we brainstormed, it could be a more natural
part of your regular conversation or standing meetings."

"It pays to know your employees. Honestly, if I recognized
them every two or three weeks in our conversations, I would still
feel successful at recognition."

"I could see that. There are guidelines and they are intended to
show that it's easier than we think. Each employee is different. But
everyone deserves consistency in recognizing their valuable work."

"I know a couple of my team members who would cringe at being recognized. Some people have a hard time taking compliments, and there are plenty of people who might feel awkward being recognized. Certainly, different approaches do come into play in a big way," said David.

"Plus, knowing your employee, for example, face-to-face might be harder for some people compared with, say, a quick email or voicemail."

"A little awkwardness is okay, no matter the reaction. Most people will still walk away feeling thrilled knowing something they did mattered. Do what works for you and that employee. But don't avoid it because it's awkward," recapped Mark. "Then be honest with yourself if you see results. Is there more you could do?"

They revisited two approaches: "Email takes longer sometimes to write than leaving a voicemail. And you want to consider whether you want a permanent document for their file, whether to copy others, and so on."

"I love the example you gave earlier for smaller types of recognition via voicemail. Do you know how easy it would be to reflect and make a phone call and leave a message thanking someone for a job well done? Especially at the end of the day, so they come into work with that message first thing."

David liked the idea of doing something that easy at the end of the day. Mindful of his never-ending demands during the day, he thought how simple it would be to do once in a while. Give it a thoughtful moment and leave a quick voicemail while walking to his car. That, he thought, would be easy yet impactful and energizing! He and Mark talked about this thinking, and both had no problem with the notion of multitasking something like this as long as the TIPSS are in play.

"I'd definitely mix it up though; if it were me, I wouldn't want a voicemail every time," said David.

"Me either."

Mark checked his phone for the time and mentioned that they had another 20 minutes. David had been thinking about rewards and was planning to make that a topic on their list in the near future, but instead suggested they use the rest of their time to mull that over.

"So, how do we know when to give a reward then, if we're saying rewards should not take over recognition and just be used once in a while?"

Mark had also been giving that some thought and had only some general benchmarking he ran across in his recognition research. He qualified, "Research is shaky. Most of it interchanges rewards with recognition with service awards or assumes rewards are given every single time. *We* are not saying that."

"Definitely not. So let's spell out what we are saying about rewards. Maybe something like guidelines or criteria."

Mark flipped the page, and with a little brainstorming, they came up with the following.

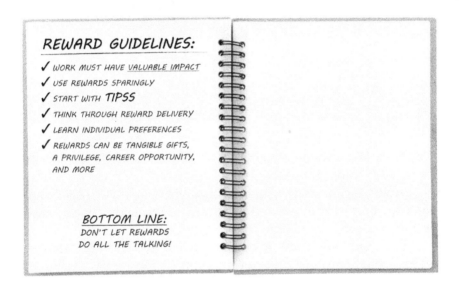

REWARD GUIDELINES:

✓ WORK MUST HAVE VALUABLE IMPACT
✓ USE REWARDS SPARINGLY
✓ START WITH TIPSS
✓ THINK THROUGH REWARD DELIVERY
✓ LEARN INDIVIDUAL PREFERENCES
✓ REWARDS CAN BE TANGIBLE GIFTS, A PRIVILEGE, CAREER OPPORTUNITY, AND MORE

BOTTOM LINE:
DON'T LET REWARDS
DO ALL THE TALKING!

After some discussion, these guidelines made sense to Mark and David. They especially felt solid on not letting the rewards do all the talking.

"At best, it's a missed opportunity for a manager to make a meaningful connection with the employee." Mark reiterated from earlier thinking, "And at its worst, it can create confusion and even mistrust or cynicism."

"The TIPSS will be what makes the reward authentic. Even though the TIPSS were written under the Reward Guidelines, he spelled them out on the next page as a reminder.

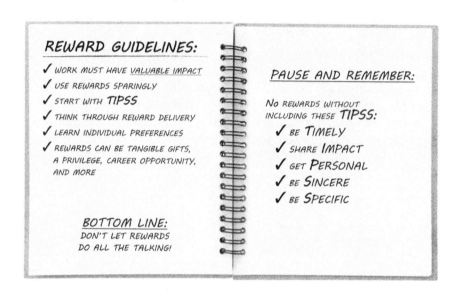

REWARD GUIDELINES:

✓ WORK MUST HAVE VALUABLE IMPACT
✓ USE REWARDS SPARINGLY
✓ START WITH TIPSS
✓ THINK THROUGH REWARD DELIVERY
✓ LEARN INDIVIDUAL PREFERENCES
✓ REWARDS CAN BE TANGIBLE GIFTS, A PRIVILEGE, CAREER OPPORTUNITY, AND MORE

BOTTOM LINE:
DON'T LET REWARDS DO ALL THE TALKING!

PAUSE AND REMEMBER:

No REWARDS WITHOUT INCLUDING THESE TIPSS:

✓ BE TIMELY
✓ SHARE IMPACT
✓ GET PERSONAL
✓ BE SINCERE
✓ BE SPECIFIC

"Nice. Rewards should never stand alone," said Mark. "Alright, that was 25 minutes but worth the extra five."

"Well worth it, and let me add that when we deliver the Lunch and Learn, let's include a section on rewards and how they can help or hurt intrinsic motivation."

"For sure! We want managers to get the message that rewards have their place, are not the same as recognition, and have guidelines."

David needed to get to his next meeting, and they planned to connect again. As they were gathering devices, they decided that their next task would be to summarize other reasons or motivations to recognize more often. But first, they have another Key Take-Away to include in the notebook.

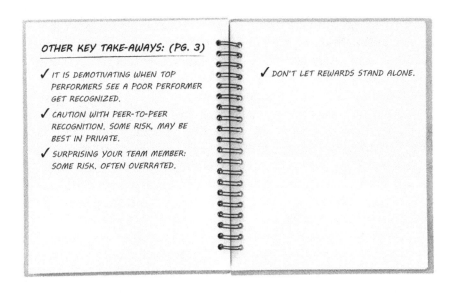

OTHER KEY TAKE-AWAYS: (PG. 3)

✓ IT IS DEMOTIVATING WHEN TOP
   PERFORMERS SEE A POOR PERFORMER
   GET RECOGNIZED.

✓ CAUTION WITH PEER-TO-PEER
   RECOGNITION. SOME RISK, MAY BE
   BEST IN PRIVATE.

✓ SURPRISING YOUR TEAM MEMBER:
   SOME RISK. OFTEN OVERRATED.

✓ DON'T LET REWARDS STAND ALONE.

Fundamental 4: Recognition Is an Invaluable Tool Available to Every Manager

"How's the salad? Liking it more now that you are changing your eating habits?"

David responded with something about people asking rude questions.

Satisfied he got the better of David for the moment, Mark turned to his lunch and changed the subject to the motivation behind recognition.

"The research is solid on recognition increasing performance, retention, and ultimately the bottom line. But, I think it's worth acknowledging more clearly the benefits to the manager."

"Let's take Donna, for example. Based on what you've told me, I'd guess it's more about the bottom line for her," ventured David.

Mark agreed that she is very bottom-line driven. "But I think, as Donna gets more experience recognizing her employees, she will see how recognition is central to them delivering to the bottom line. In fact, I think that may be true for most of us, honestly. She believes that the reason Ajay left at all—or this soon—was because he didn't feel the impactful work he did was valued. To be clear, there could have been several factors as to why he left."

"It's rarely one reason," David agreed.

"True, but for someone on the fence, or someone in the 'I can't lose this person' category—and maybe that's Ajay—sometimes authentic recognition is enough to retain someone."

Agreeing that retention was something managers could influence far more, they went back to what else is motivating beyond the bottom line.

"From what I know of Donna, she would be very skilled at bringing the bottom line into recognition eventually, regardless of motivation," David said.

"She has really mentored me in this area. Donna hasn't met a process, model, measure, or scorecard that she hasn't loved. And still, for her, I'm certain the reward is that feeling we talked about—pride of being a great leader who can motivate a team, who can inspire loyalty and all that goes with it. And frankly, maybe I'm just talking about myself because that is the truth. What manager out there wouldn't feel great about that?"

"Most managers want to be great managers. And once they are great managers, they become great leaders."

"So, lots of motivations to recognize, and all good reasons. Some we've already talked about, but I want to get it down in one area. Hand over the notebook."

David drew this diagram of their thoughts in the notebook.

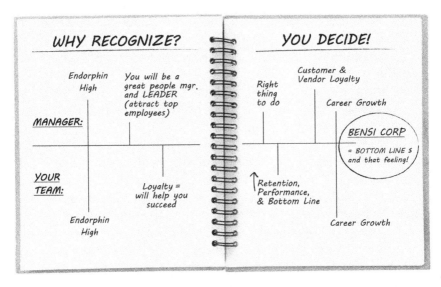

"We could think of several more; what I like is that there is a motivation for nearly everyone. Some are motivated by growing careers. For others, recognition is simply the right thing to do. Some managers feel something like a buzz from it. And, of course, for others, it's more about the bottom line," said David.

"And, of course, our customers are impacted by our bottom line. That is another reason, right? Recognition can have longer arms than just internal to Bensi Corp. How about business to business? I work with our vendors all the time, and we have a good professional relationship. What if I used the TIPSS with them too? Not to get them to do something for me but for similar reasons with our team members. It is the right thing to do, and the better the relationship, the better their performance for us and possibly the more loyal they may be."

"Good point. Last week one of my vendors raised an issue for something she simply wanted me to be aware of. I thanked her profusely and chalked it up to a good relationship. But why not let our vendor know when they do a good job? Untold benefits to all of us and our bottom line."

"That is the serious business of all of this. No matter your motivation for recognizing consistently, it affects the bottom line."

"For me, it's competition. I want to be better than any other manager and therefore be a better leader. So I'm motivated to be more consistent with recognition. I do like the quest, though, of the bottom line as it is sustainable only with a motivated team. It can really be crummy when your team is not thrilled to be at work," said David.

"There are more reasons for me for sure, but I gotta say the endorphin high has me at hello."

"Stephen probably gets an endorphin high even with his one-size-fits-all approach. He may believe that he is doing a good job with his team," David said.

"And honestly, in that way Stephen is like many managers—most have not been taught. Hence the Lunch and Learn notion."

David wasn't convinced that Stephen would be interested in learning. He did think that there are a lot of 'Jans' in the work world—someone who has a lot to offer and is slightly in a rut without support. David added that he would love to see Jan take more ownership and pull herself out of it. He did expect more from a senior buyer, if he is honest. Either way, she needs a nudge, and it will help everyone. *Or*, better, if managers like Jan turned it around for their teams and recognized their work consistently, it would help a lot. Pointing back at the picture he just drew in the notebook, David emphasized that they could benefit in many other ways. He admitted that he is already learning not to wait around for Stephen. David knows he can give his team kudos with or without Stephen.

"Donna and I are going to keep talking about this topic. She said she is fine with my sharing some of our more personal conversations with you. I think she is on to me. I expect she knows that we talk; I probably would be sharing them anyway!"

"She also knows that between you and me, it stays in the vault. I really appreciate Donna's trust and her support of the Lunch and Learn," said David.

Flipping back to the Recognition Fundamentals page, Mark told David what he had in mind and with David's agreement, wrote down the fourth Fundamental:

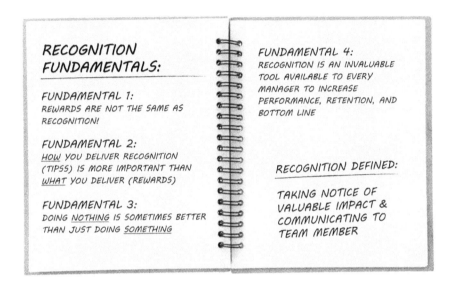

RECOGNITION FUNDAMENTALS:

FUNDAMENTAL 1:
REWARDS ARE NOT THE SAME AS RECOGNITION!

FUNDAMENTAL 2:
HOW YOU DELIVER RECOGNITION (TIPSS) IS MORE IMPORTANT THAN WHAT YOU DELIVER (REWARDS)

FUNDAMENTAL 3:
DOING NOTHING IS SOMETIMES BETTER THAN JUST DOING SOMETHING

FUNDAMENTAL 4:
RECOGNITION IS AN INVALUABLE TOOL AVAILABLE TO EVERY MANAGER TO INCREASE PERFORMANCE, RETENTION, AND BOTTOM LINE

RECOGNITION DEFINED:

TAKING NOTICE OF VALUABLE IMPACT & COMMUNICATING TO TEAM MEMBER

They vetted these Fundamentals a little more and squared it with the thinking they have done so far.

Thinking more personally about the four Fundamentals, David said, "And of course, our employees should not be viewed as our kids, but I can see how the four Fundamentals apply when I praise my kids. There's a different bottom line we go for; it's not financial. It's more about their own pride and growth. If I were to say, 'Hey Lucas, nice work on your essay. The example you provided on the Grand Canyon, and your data about rainfall really gave it credibility.' I am certain that approach would inspire meaning and pride. I believe in that regard, that kind of bottom line would be very relatable and motivating with our employees too!"

"Love the thinking, and it drives home that it's not always bottom line motivated. I can see a future Lunch and Learn you could lead on family recognition. I don't know about you, but my experience is that the more we personalize our business learnings, the more we are likely to use them to their full potential. I recall taking a communications course, and that has helped me personally in countless ways."

"Let me get a handle on this first, but it has me reflecting on how and when I praise my kids. And now I see why Rebecca is really good at it."

Mark urged him not to lose sight of that and thought there was real value there. "After all, your kids need to be someone's co-workers someday!"

"Exactly. Let's add another Key Take-Away before we go."

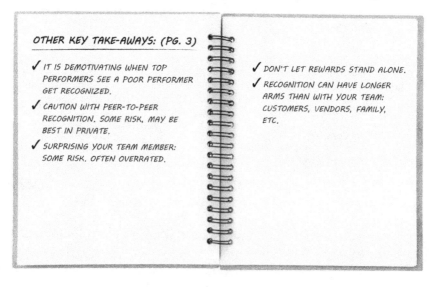

OTHER KEY TAKE-AWAYS: (PG. 3)

✓ IT IS DEMOTIVATING WHEN TOP PERFORMERS SEE A POOR PERFORMER GET RECOGNIZED.

✓ CAUTION WITH PEER-TO-PEER RECOGNITION. SOME RISK, MAY BE BEST IN PRIVATE.

✓ SURPRISING YOUR TEAM MEMBER: SOME RISK. OFTEN OVERRATED.

✓ DON'T LET REWARDS STAND ALONE.

✓ RECOGNITION CAN HAVE LONGER ARMS THAN WITH YOUR TEAM: CUSTOMERS, VENDORS, FAMILY, ETC.

Objections

DAVID: I have objections.

MARK: Okay, I'll bite.

...thinking more about why we don't recognize. You know, barriers. Objections!

Got it.

(I'm ignoring your attention-seeking opening)

Not sure what to do with them, but I want to talk about objections a bit.

I followed up with Jan and have some input from her.

I also talked with other managers.

I'm sending meeting notice.

Fine. Next week I have more one-hour openings.

One week later, Mark and David were seated at a table in the atrium.

"Let's address obstacles that managers may have to recognizing consistently. There are some more traditional barrier points such as no time, no budget, didn't know they should, and so on," suggested David.

"Let's also address the notion that managers just don't know how and that it might feel awkward, to name two more."

Mark asked David what Jan had to say about why she or other managers don't recognize effectively or enough.

"Similar obstacles: doesn't come naturally, easier to do nothing, no time."

"I got similar feedback."

"One thing Jan pointed out was that since Stephen doesn't recognize her, she doesn't think about recognizing her team. She also included obstacles such as lack of budget, awkwardness, and that people shouldn't be rewarded just to do their jobs."

"Lots to address. The 'time' objection seems like a common one. I wonder if sometimes when people say they don't have time, what they're really saying is 'I don't have time to figure out how' versus 'I don't have time to take one minute to recognize.' This is the reason we are simplifying and making it easy—to take 'time' off the table," said Mark.

"Good points. The 'why should I reward people just for doing their job' objection is one I related to before we started talking about this topic. I do believe that often—and I wish it were always—we get what we expect from people."

"Meaning?"

"Do your job. If I expect people to do their job, great. They might meet expectations all day long. Maybe that's fine, but why low-ball it? Especially since I am buying into the payoff when we recognize impact."

"Well said."

That was a lot to address. As they thought about some of the objections, it helped them confirm why it was important to have a recognition definition along with the TIPSS.

"Working with Jan, even a little, and getting her input seemed to energize her. I think she's letting go of expecting differently from Stephen. It's her reality. But it's been cool, and she brought up several more thoughts. She does want to be involved and wants to see all managers have some kind of training and even joked about Stephen not 'getting it' even if he did participate. It's good to see her have a little more spring in her step. Not being thrilled with her manager hopefully won't stop her from wanting to do well with her team."

"That is great! We can use all those objections she identified when we do the Lunch and Learn."

Mark had an idea to capture all of the objections they've talked about. In the spirit of recognition transparency, they would publish them. The list would be intended as something to be added to and used for educating: webinars, blogs, bulletin boards, Lunch and Learns, and other methods.

Mark got out his laptop and started the objections list. They collected as many as they could think of. They would write the answers another time. For now, they compiled the list as the first pass from their brainstorm and information collected from other managers.

Potential Objections
- I don't have time for recognition.
- I'm not sure what to do. I might get it wrong.
- Recognizing feels awkward for my employee and me.
- I have no recognition budget.
- People like rewards. They're not complaining.
- What if we don't have turnover? Maybe consistent recognition is not necessary?
- We already have a recognition program. What then?
- What if executives are not on board?
- What about me? My boss doesn't recognize me.
- Should poor or mediocre performers be recognized?
- Won't people call foul if they see others getting recognized more than they are?
- Isn't it like giving everyone a trophy?
- Isn't it their job to do their job?
- They already get service awards. Isn't that enough?
- Diversity of heritage, age, culture, background---how does these tie in?

"Okay, good. Objections recorded."

"Too many to put in the notebook. It's good to see the main objections all together so I can grasp what we've explored," suggested David.

"Our exploration wasn't so simple, but we can claim that our answers to these objections will attempt to be," added Mark. "So let's go!"

"Let's add another Key-Take Away first."

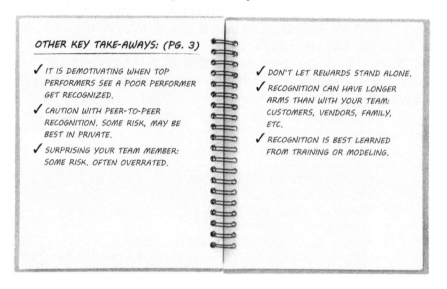

OTHER KEY TAKE-AWAYS: (PG. 3)

✓ *IT IS DEMOTIVATING WHEN TOP PERFORMERS SEE A POOR PERFORMER GET RECOGNIZED.*

✓ *CAUTION WITH PEER-TO-PEER RECOGNITION. SOME RISK, MAY BE BEST IN PRIVATE.*

✓ *SURPRISING YOUR TEAM MEMBER: SOME RISK. OFTEN OVERRATED.*

✓ *DON'T LET REWARDS STAND ALONE.*

✓ *RECOGNITION CAN HAVE LONGER ARMS THAN WITH YOUR TEAM: CUSTOMERS, VENDORS, FAMILY, ETC.*

✓ *RECOGNITION IS BEST LEARNED FROM TRAINING OR MODELING.*

The Notebook Lunch and Learn: Recognition Rebooted

Armed with their notebook, Mark and David pulled their thinking together. They summarized all their main ideas and developed it into their Lunch and Learn outline. Here is what they included:

Bensi Corp Lunch and Learn: Recognition Rebooted

Why Recognition Matters
- Recognition often ineffective or not occurring.
- Statistics on retention, increasing performance, and bottom line.
- Managers expected to be naturally skilled at recognition, even though often not modeled or trained.
- From manager to leader.

What Recognition Is and What It Isn't

- It's not that big of a mystery.
- Definition: Taking notice of valuable impact and communicating it to the team member.

- The Four Fundamentals of Recognition:
  - F1: Rewards Are Not the Same as Recognition
  - F2: How You Deliver Recognition Is More Important Than What You Deliver
  - F3: Doing Nothing Is Sometimes Better Than Doing Something
  - F4: Recognition is an Invaluable Tool Available to Every Manager

How to Deliver Recognition

- The Essential TIPSS:
  - Be Timely
  - Discuss Impact
  - Get Personal
  - Be Sincere
  - Be Specific
- Delivery Approaches
  - Check preferences with team member.
  - In person, voicemail, public, private, group, etc.
  - Caution with public delivery approaches—especially public and peer recognition.
- Recognition and Reward Guidelines
- Recognition Objections: Overruled

Other Key Take-Aways

With the outline ready to go, Mark and David quickly developed their full Lunch and Learn program intended for all managers. With a little advertising, they delivered the first session with merchandising managers. It was well attended, and the feedback was encouraging. It included plenty of practice time with examples. They found it rewarding to see other managers as guest presenters speaking of their personal experiences. They even had employees provide testimonials from when they've experienced authentic recognition.

In addition, they wanted to address that, similar to them, the manager participants may discover that they could have been delivering recognition differently and better in the past. Mark and David were quick to offer their own reflective learnings, that intentions count and giving oneself a break can be a very productive way to pave the path forward for learning and adjusting our own leadership behavior.

David encouraged Jan that after attending the first session, she partner with him to deliver these periodically. Mark was happy to relinquish the lead role on that and participate as a guest facilitator. They thought they could add as they go, building in practice sessions. Laura, who has been finding her stride, has been very helpful and has done the internal marketing to other managers and executives with strong HR support.

They agreed to approach the Lunch and Learn as "grass roots" style versus a mandate from HR. Other managers expressed interest in participating as well, which Mark and David found encouraging. They felt that with that approach—involving other managers—they could keep the Lunch and Learn sessions more agile. They can also start to formally measure outcomes.

After some tweaking, another well attended Lunch and Learn was delivered three weeks later, open to other leaders at Bensi Corp's corporate offices, with enthusiastic participation. The Lunch and Learns were repeated every month with fresh testimonials coming from employees and managers. Several managers have claimed that their teams seem more positive and productive and that they boosted their own leadership skills. Keeping the team's impact in the forefront of communication has made a nice difference. Their goal continues to be that this Lunch and Learn would complement and, who knows, even reboot the existing recognition program at Bensi Corp.

The Scoop at Bensi Corp

The year ended well. The plans for prototyping the smaller stores in the highly populated areas were on target for next year, and

Bensi Corp was growing their employee base. Mark and David continued their recognition conversations and increased their frequency to include recognition as part of their standing meetings. Donna has recognized her team more as well.

The employee survey results were very encouraging. The organization moved the needle forward on the "feeling valued and appreciated" category, especially with the individual manager results. Donna was especially eager to see those results for the organization, as well as for herself. With promising results indicating increased engagement, the leadership team is learning that, with the employee growth plan, the best place to look is their existing employee base.

A survey comment from her team made her especially proud: "Donna appreciates my work and isn't shy about telling me. I always know where I stand, and it makes me want to perform better, hold others accountable, and grow the organization together." What more could she ask for? Donna is proud of how she has grown from leading a department to leading people to performance. She has never loved her job more. She knows she may not be able to keep all of her key managers forever, but she also knows she has better people manager tools to do her best. And they will be better for it too, no matter where they end up, benefiting Bensi Corp, her team members, and Donna herself. Us, you, me—Donna's favorite winning combination.

David was a little nervous about his survey results before he saw them. He worked hard to show appreciation to his team, and teaching the Lunch and Learns helped him model that behavior. He too was very proud to see an increase this year in his manager ratings from the survey, especially in his team feeling appreciated. He is crystal clear now that a rating like that means more than a warm fuzzy feeling. It is a predictor of how engaged his team is to perform well and stay with Bensi Corp. He feels like a better leader and will carry that forward whatever role he is in.

Jan continues to feel the benefits of increasing the recognition to her team members when they add value. While she has more ground to cover, she is very pleased with her slight increase in favorable ratings from her team. The ratings have helped her feel more energized and validated for the authentic effort she has made in recognizing her team. The end of quarter report showed a small increase in her team's productivity. It's too early to make the direct link, but she does know this is a better way for her to operate.

Jan also realized that for a long time she'd been waiting for her manager, Stephen, to become a good people manager. She understands now that waiting for Stephen is unproductive. Having an ineffective manager is a reality sometimes and doesn't mean she can't be a great manager to her own team. She has four employees who are especially high performers, and while she is not ignoring the other productive team members, she is intentionally focused on making sure their incredible value is clear to them. Influencing where she can with no guarantees, she feels more in control than she ever has in her job.

With the quarter over and the weekend ahead, there were so many conversations rolling around in Mark's mind. Tipping the employee survey scale with employees feeling more valued and recognized and a continued enjoyable work relationship with Donna were only a couple. And, of course, the recognition project. Mark knew that there is a book in all of this that will include the ideas and thoughts he, David, and Donna have collected over the past year. He also knows that he need not go further than their own office to tell the story. A book, he thought. Expand on the notebook. That could be interesting.

* * * * *

Seven Measly Minutes

MARK: It's been three years since Ajay left!

DAVID: That was fast! That event was our inspiration for our recognition project as I like to call it.

Lots has happened. Donna continues to lead in more people-oriented ways.

I retired my cape.

and ACQUIRED a promotion.

Can't wait to transition! Thanks in large part to Donna mentoring.

Plus, a book.

We already had the material for it. That was both of us with help from many others, especially Donna.

True, though you made it into a real live book. It's been good pre-reading for the Lunch and Learn.

Hope so! My monthly question: So how is Softlines? (Speaking of promotions)

Can't believe I've been in Stephen's role a year already. More and more I realize he wasn't long for Bensi Corp. I will actually miss that large personality.

Me too, in an entertaining kind of way. Leave it to him to wrangle regular guest spots on Morning USA. People love him. Seems he used his time well on all those visits to our Manhattan stores.

Ha! I love this role. A stretch, but good. Helped that Sebastian and I revamped it to play to my strengths. Jan's flourishing. She will be ready for her next move this year.

Good to see her thriving.

I expect she doesn't miss the tie rejects.

We laugh now!

I'll deny this in public, but you really did help me a lot in building a team, keeping my high performers.

Well it's a mutual deal. You got me into Bensi Corp, all our recognition conversations, etc. We're even.

Fair enough. We're both doing well.

So all those humiliating times mom dropped us off at the school bus shouting "make good choices" paid off!

Except during that awkward time I call adolescence, it must have done some good.

I was too busy being awkward to notice.

And in spite of that – you're still mom's fav. You get the first call with all the family news.

We've been through this. First born deserves that privilege.

Seven measly minutes do not make you my elder and I continue to stand by that.

Listen up – no matter who's wiser (me), who's older (me again).

No matter who's better at the stock market (me) or who's a better tennis player (duh, me).

Alright, channeling mom – what would she say? There's enough room for both of us to be recognized and feel valued. Awwww!!

Well amen, brother!

Epilogue

Ajay left his table and walked toward the door just as Donna entered the restaurant. Many thoughts came swirling at her. After all she's learned, she now thinks she knows why he left and, better, what she could have done differently to possibly keep him at Bensi Corp. Ajay's resignation gave her much to think about, and with all her research and careful planning, there was one area that she knew she overlooked in the past: letting her employees know how valuable it is when their work makes an impact. Recognition.

There was a time when she thought a new promotion or job title or bonus was all anyone ever needed to feel valued. She also knows career development is a big motivator for many employees. And that was especially important to Ajay given how quickly and eagerly he moved through Bensi Corp. She now believes that, for some employees, it is more than those things.

Donna caught Ajay's eye, and his face lit up. With a big smile, she couldn't resist telling him that he graduated from "Golden Child" and is now affectionately known as "the one who got away." After a few exchanges about how they were each doing, Donna decided to ask him directly—to confirm what she thought—as to why he left.

Ajay shared that he was less focused on why he chose to leave and more centered on where he was going. This new job seemed to be more visible, and since a friend highly recommended the company, he thought that his skills would be valued there. He explained that it was no reflection on Donna; he believed Donna appreciated his work and emphasized to her that it wasn't that he was unhappy.

He explained to Donna that it wasn't until he was in the process of exploring his new job, and more so in these past three years in it, that he could reflect on why he didn't feel loyal to Bensi Corp. "I really liked Bensi Corp, and it wasn't that I was disgruntled. It was more that I was drawn to an organization where most of the leaders recognized the value of the individual contributions consistently and in many ways, even if there was no clear roadmap for my next job title."

Ajay commented that the sole focus at Bensi Corp seemed to be promotions—something super important to him—but it grew thin when there were few conversations and appreciation of the value he brings. Still, he was grateful for the promotions, a reward for his hard work. It just didn't help him feel loyal when the conversations didn't match the promotions. It left him with a feeling of having more of a transactional experience. Donna could see that it probably wasn't that fulfilling to him to have promotions without truly recognizing his impact over the long term. He emphasized his gratitude to Donna for helping champion his career and gratitude for his promotions.

Donna understood. This confirmed what she thought, and it helped provide closure for her. She was so happy to see Ajay energized. She told him that she was thrilled for his new job and that it was an important learning experience for all of them. She shared that recognizing employees does not mean it has to be a big tangible reward like a promotion or bonus. That it doesn't need to be formal and complicated. More part of regular conversations.

Ajay had a big grin on his face as he listened to Donna's reflections. When she asked why he was smiling, he said, "It's so good to see you not overcomplicate this! Plus, I'm reading Mark's book. I recognize some people in there!" They both laughed and agreed it was great running into each other. Donna thanked him for his honesty and the outstanding work he did at Bensi Corp that continues to be incorporated by the team, and thanks in part to Ajay's legacy, the department is poised for success.

Appendix A – Quick Employee Recognition Tools

Quick Tool: How Do You Wish to Be Recognized?

Don't guess. Ask your team member. Completing this form together can open up a great conversation. In addition, you as a manager will better understand your team member's preferences, enabling successful recognition. Keep this in the employee's file and check in periodically to see if preferences change. Your team member will welcome this!

Team Member's Name:

You Might Say to Your Team Member: *My intention is to reflect back to you on a more consistent basis when your work shows special value and has an impact. I want to make sure that I understand your preferences so that when I recognize your work, it can be most successful for both of us.*

Approach: Circle any of the approaches that would be okay with you.
- Face-to-face
- Voicemail
- Handwritten note
- Email just to you
- Email and copy key people
- Public recognition in front of small group or large group
- Others?

Questions for Your Team Member: Is there a part of your work that you believe makes a difference or that you especially wish to be recognized for?

If a reward is included in recognition, what are your preferences? For example, gift cards, cash, specific gifts, food items, etc. Or if you like to be surprised, please list some of your hobbies or interests to help spark some ideas for me.

Are there other things important to you that I should know about when it comes to recognition? Things you fear? Things you have seen that you liked?

Quick Tool: Practice Recognizing Impactful Work

Practice Verbal Recognition: Don't wing it. Give it a quick practice. Practice by yourself or with a trusted colleague. Some managers record it in their phones and listen back to see how it sounds. Whatever method you want to try, take a minute to prepare what you will say. This will help your recognition delivery be more successful for everyone.

Lead with Your Intentions: Explain why you are talking with the person or why you are leaving the voicemail.

Example: *I want to recognize you for helping me with the proposal. I don't mean to catch you off guard, but you deserve to know how much you helped me last week.*

Practice Delivery Essentials TIPSS in Any Order

- Be **T**imely. Don't delay, though it is never too late.
- Discuss **I**mpact. What impact did this have for you, someone else, or the organization that was valuable?
- Get **P**ersonal. Don't be generic. Tell how this was unique to this person's skill set.
- Be **S**incere. Sometimes when we feel uncomfortable, we make jokes or use verbal fillers. Just be truthful, and you will sound sincere.
- Be **S**pecific. State specifically what the person has done that was impactful.

Example: *Thank you, Joseph, for stepping in and developing the agenda for our meeting on Thursday. Being out on vacation, I felt out of the loop. The best part was that you really seemed tapped into the last two weeks' work cycle. This made for a far better agenda, and, in fact, the last two items that I hadn't considered really pushed us forward in making decisions then and there, rather than waiting for the next meeting. We saved a few days and lots of back and forth communication. Awesome job and really helpful! Thank you, Joseph!*

Quick Tool: Plan the Recognition Conversation

Team Member's Name:

Approach:

Recognized for:

Use TIPSS to Plan:

- Be Timely:

- Discuss Impact:

- Get Personal:

- Be Sincere:

- Be Specific:

Jot it down using TIPSS:

Appendix B – Four Main Responses to Recognition

What about the other side of Recognition? Receiving recognition. Employees' past experiences can influence their reactions to receiving praise. As a manager, you may be surprised and even frustrated when you happily offer praise and an individual receives it awkwardly. Being aware of and prepared for various reactions can help ensure that the recognition is still successful. From my research, I have distilled four main types of responses to receiving recognition.

- Cool Response—Takes compliments well, may simply thank you, internally agrees, and is comfortable with the recognition. Delivering recognition to a person who has this type of response is usually very easy.
- Crave Response—Can't get enough praise. This employee often seeks affirmation with questions such as, "How was that deliverable?" "Did I present okay in the meeting?" "Does the team like me?" Bring on the recognition! This person is waiting for you.
- Cautious Response—Believes you have another agenda when you offer praise. "What do you want from me?" is a common reaction. Be specific in your example so this employee believes you. Starting with "I would like to recognize you for something . . ." can also offer reassurance that you have no hidden agenda.
- Cringe Response—Is uncomfortable being in the spotlight, even if the recognition is in private. Typically, this employee deflects, downplays, or dismisses the praise, which can be especially frustrating. When this occurs, simply ending the conversation with, "You deserve to know that your work made an impact," can be helpful.

All of these responses can be normal. Do be mindful about public versus private recognition. Public recognition for someone who dislikes it can very quickly turn a Cool response into a Cringe response. In addition, don't let the Cringe and Cautious responses stop you. While an employee may be caught off guard, once the awkward moment has passed, your words may be remembered with pleasure and pride, even if in the moment it may not seem that way. While some managers are skilled at continuously coaching their team members in interpersonal communication, it isn't a manager's responsibility to control the employee's reaction to recognition. Offering recognition *is* part of your job as a manager, and being mindful and prepared for common reactions is kind, professional, and honest, all of which build trust in you as a manager.

Appendix C – The Notebook Condensed

RECOGNITION FUNDAMENTALS:

FUNDAMENTAL 1:
REWARDS ARE NOT THE SAME AS RECOGNITION!

FUNDAMENTAL 2:
HOW YOU DELIVER RECOGNITION (TIPSS) IS MORE IMPORTANT THAN _WHAT_ YOU DELIVER (REWARDS)

FUNDAMENTAL 3:
DOING _NOTHING_ IS SOMETIMES BETTER THAN JUST DOING _SOMETHING_

FUNDAMENTAL 4:
RECOGNITION IS AN INVALUABLE TOOL AVAILABLE TO EVERY MANAGER TO INCREASE PERFORMANCE, RETENTION, AND BOTTOM LINE

RECOGNITION DEFINED:

TAKING NOTICE OF VALUABLE IMPACT & COMMUNICATING TO TEAM MEMBER

RECOGNITION DELIVERY ESSENTIALS:

TIPSS TO INCLUDE:
(ANY ORDER)
- ✓ BE TIMELY
- ✓ DISCUSS IMPACT*
- ✓ GET PERSONAL
- ✓ BE SINCERE
- ✓ BE SPECIFIC

SMALL EFFORT - **BIG** PAYOFF!

THE MORE TIPSS YOU USE EACH TIME, THE BETTER PAYOFF FOR PERFORMANCE, RETENTION, AND BOTTOM LINE

*IMPACT = SOMETIMES YOU EXPECT IT TO HAVE IMPACT, BUT MAY NOT KNOW WHAT THAT IS JUST YET

BIZ PAYOFF:

INCREASE PERFORMANCE, RETENTION, AND BOTTOM LINE

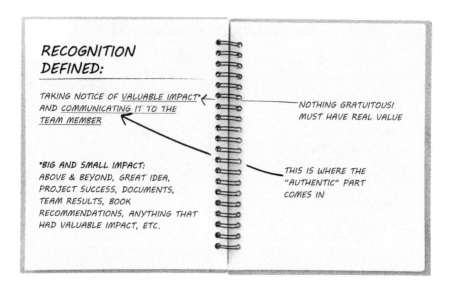

RECOGNITION DEFINED:

TAKING NOTICE OF <u>VALUABLE IMPACT</u>* AND <u>COMMUNICATING IT TO THE TEAM MEMBER</u>

*BIG AND SMALL IMPACT: ABOVE & BEYOND, GREAT IDEA, PROJECT SUCCESS, DOCUMENTS, TEAM RESULTS, BOOK RECOMMENDATIONS, ANYTHING THAT HAD VALUABLE IMPACT, ETC.

NOTHING GRATUITOUS! MUST HAVE REAL VALUE

THIS IS WHERE THE "AUTHENTIC" PART COMES IN

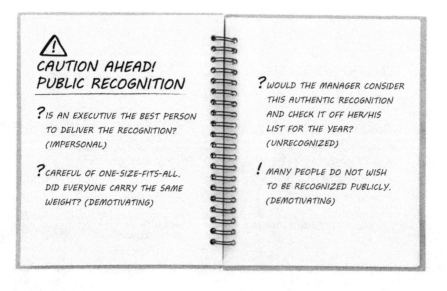

⚠️ CAUTION AHEAD! PUBLIC RECOGNITION

? IS AN EXECUTIVE THE BEST PERSON TO DELIVER THE RECOGNITION? (IMPERSONAL)

? CAREFUL OF ONE-SIZE-FITS-ALL. DID EVERYONE CARRY THE SAME WEIGHT? (DEMOTIVATING)

? WOULD THE MANAGER CONSIDER THIS AUTHENTIC RECOGNITION AND CHECK IT OFF HER/HIS LIST FOR THE YEAR? (UNRECOGNIZED)

! MANY PEOPLE DO NOT WISH TO BE RECOGNIZED PUBLICLY. (DEMOTIVATING)

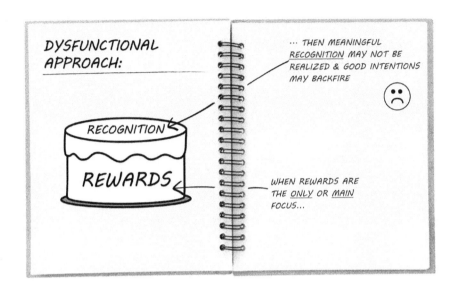

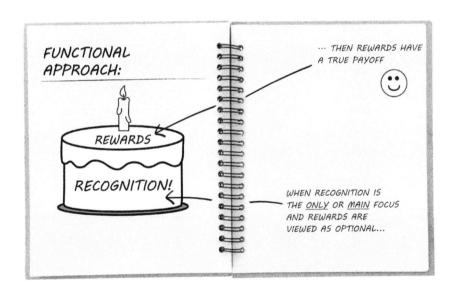

RECOGNITION DELIVERY APPROACHES:

- ✓ IN PERSON →
- ✓ VOICEMAIL →
- ✓ HAND-WRITTEN NOTE →
- ✓ EMAIL →
- ✓ LARGE/SMALL GROUP →
- ✓ PUBLIC OR PRIVATE →
- ✓ ETC.

CONSIDER:

(DON'T SCARE THEM!)
(STAND ALONE!)
(REMEMBER THOSE?)
(DELIBERATE SUBJECT LINE)
(WHO SHOULD WITNESS THIS?)
(ARE THEY PRIVATE OR SHY?)

RECOGNITION DELIVERY CONSIDERATIONS:

- ✓ EVERY WEEK OR TWO, PER EMPLOYEE AS PART OF REGULAR CONVERSATIONS (ASSUMING WORK HAS VALUABLE IMPACT)

- ✓ 5% OF MANAGER TIME SPENT ON RECOGNITION (LARGER IMPACT = LARGER REWARD)

- ✓ BUDGET 1-2% PAYROLL (THE FEW SELECT TIMES WE CHOOSE TO REWARD)

NOT A SCIENCE!
DO WHAT MAKES SENSE FOR YOU

(BECAUSE SOME PEOPLE WANT PARAMETERS)

REWARD GUIDELINES:

✓ WORK MUST HAVE <u>VALUABLE IMPACT</u>
✓ USE REWARDS SPARINGLY
✓ START WITH TIPSS
✓ THINK THROUGH REWARD DELIVERY
✓ LEARN INDIVIDUAL PREFERENCES
✓ REWARDS CAN BE TANGIBLE GIFTS, A PRIVILEGE, CAREER OPPORTUNITY, AND MORE

PAUSE AND REMEMBER:

No REWARDS WITHOUT INCLUDING THESE TIPSS:

✓ BE TIMELY
✓ SHARE IMPACT
✓ GET PERSONAL
✓ BE SINCERE
✓ BE SPECIFIC

BOTTOM LINE:
DON'T LET REWARDS DO ALL THE TALKING!

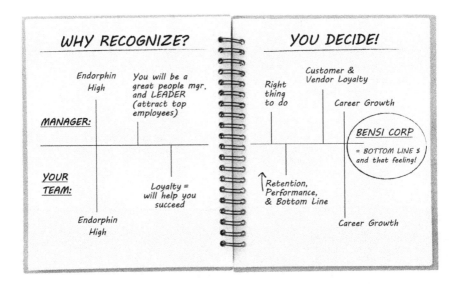

WHY RECOGNIZE?

MANAGER:

Endorphin High | You will be a great people mgr. and LEADER (attract top employees)

YOUR TEAM:

Loyalty = will help you succeed

Endorphin High

YOU DECIDE!

Right thing to do | Customer & Vendor Loyalty

Career Growth

BENSI CORP

= BOTTOM LINE $ and that feeling!

↑ Retention, Performance, & Bottom Line

Career Growth

OTHER KEY TAKE-AWAYS:

✓ MANAGERS FOCUS ON FIXING THINGS; LEADERS ALSO FOCUS ON WHAT'S GOING WELL.

✓ FOR MEDIOCRE PERFORMANCE WITH FULL EFFORT, RECOGNIZE EFFORT VS THE WORK. (PRIVATELY)

✓ BEFORE INDIV. MEETINGS, ESPECIALLY WITH HIGH PERFORMERS, TELL THEM ONE THING THAT THEY DID THAT HAD VALUABLE IMPACT.

✓ DON'T NEED TO TAKE ON THE WORLD. DON'T NEED TO TRANSFORM THE WHOLE ORG. JUST THINK GLOBALLY, ACT LOCALLY, AND START WITH YOUR TEAM.

✓ $$ NOT REQUIRED TO RECOGNIZE.

✓ YOU DON'T HAVE TO BE A NATURAL. IT'S OKAY TO FEEL AWKWARD.

OTHER KEY TAKE-AWAYS: (PG. 3)

✓ IT IS DEMOTIVATING WHEN TOP PERFORMERS SEE A POOR PERFORMER GET RECOGNIZED.

✓ CAUTION WITH PEER-TO-PEER RECOGNITION. SOME RISK, MAY BE BEST IN PRIVATE.

✓ SURPRISING YOUR TEAM MEMBER: SOME RISK. OFTEN OVERRATED.

✓ DON'T LET REWARDS STAND ALONE.

✓ RECOGNITION CAN HAVE LONGER ARMS THAN WITH YOUR TEAM: CUSTOMERS, VENDORS, FAMILY, ETC.

✓ RECOGNITION IS BEST LEARNED FROM TRAINING OR MODELING.

Appendix D – Recognition Objections: Overruled!

I don't have time for recognition. If you are still reinventing recognition every time—trying to figure out how to approach it, digging around for paperwork, determining how much you have to spend on a reward, then deciding the reward, and then deciding on the reward—then you may be right. That takes a lot of time and energy. To make it easier for every manager, I invite you to consider the simpler and *more effective approach* outlined in this book. Ask yourself: Do I have a few minutes per employee to let them know the impact they are having, especially if it leads to increased performance and less turnover? You may find that you do have the time.

I'm not sure what to do. I might get it wrong. Most of us are not naturals at recognition. It's possible that you might get recognition "wrong" to some degree. No one wants to do something they aren't going to be good at. But give yourself a break and increase your skills with recognition. Learning how to recognize others is best when modeled well or with training. If you have not been trained in delivering recognition, as most managers have not, then the TIPSS are a great way to start. Practice with someone you trust, or record yourself on your smartphone first—whatever method you choose. Don't wing it! Take 30 seconds to think through the TIPSS, and you will be fine and the intention will count, especially if you tell your team of your plan to recognize their work more often.

Recognizing feels awkward for my employee and me. Yes, you are right; it can be awkward. Let the person know your intention is not to embarrass him or her. If you wait until you don't feel awkward, you may never recognize. I promise, though, it will get easier as you gain the courage to recognize your team members, and the awkwardness may even lessen or go away. You may eventually even look forward to the conversation.

I have no recognition budget. That's even better. Rewards are not the same as authentic recognition and can lead to critical missed opportunities for the manager. Instead, focus on recognizing your team member by earnestly communicating the impact she or he has had without thinking of the reward first. It is more effective to authentically recognize your team member and *then* use rewards sparingly and deliberately. *Recognition should come from you, not the Finance Department's budget.*

People like rewards. They're not complaining. If given a reward, most of us will gladly accept it. But a reward, without telling each person why they received it and how their work impacted the organization, falls flat and will not likely get the results you are looking for.

What if we don't have turnover? Maybe consistent recognition is not necessary? You are fortunate. Perhaps. Are there team members who you really want to retain? If they were to leave the organization, will you benefit if they are still your ally? Are there team members who you would *prefer* to leave your organization? Are there team members who might be performing better if they were more motivated? Do you want to be a very effective people manager? Do you wish to increase your leadership skills? If you answered yes to any of these questions, then consistent recognition is necessary.

We already have a recognition program. What then? Does it work well? Is it contributing to increased engagement, motivation, and performance? You are not required to use the program to let your team member know that performance is impactful. If you are feeling energetic, try recognizing your team more often and see your results. Then partner with HR to find ways that the company program may be adjusted.

What if executives are not on board? Focus on impacting your team whether or not executives are on board. In some organizations, getting executive buy-in can be a tall order. Do you need all the executives on board to tell a team member that her or his work is impactful? Show some value in this area, then see if that gets executive attention if you choose to broaden the recognition message.

What about me? My boss doesn't recognize me. Rising above this may perhaps define you as a leader. If this is your reality, ask yourself: How productive is it for me to wait around for my manager to recognize me? How productive is it for me to withhold recognition for those who deserve it?

Should poor or mediocre performers be recognized? Recognition is situational. Every manager's job is to treat their team members as individuals, not as a large singular unit. Ask yourself why the person is a poor or mediocre performer. Is the person performing this way yet trying exceedingly hard? Then praise the *effort* but not the work. Be truthful. This may help the person gain confidence and skills. If the person is not performing well, and not giving much effort, then no, do not recognize the work or the effort. That may sound harsh, but to do so could be demotivating and confusing to your other performers.

Won't people call foul if they see others getting recognized more than they are? They might. Assuming you are recognizing for valuable impact sincerely, welcome that conversation with any team member! What a great chance to explain why others have been recognized and how to get more recognition. Being transparent about it is healthy. As a reminder, managers will do well to consider the cautions on public recognition.

Isn't it like giving everyone a trophy? When you recognize everyone at the same time for the same thing, it is. When you individualize it and use the TIPSS, then you are off to a very effective start. Remember, a valuable impact is required to qualify for recognition.

Isn't it their job to do their job? Yes. And it is a manager's job to manage people. Employees deserve to know when their work has great impact. Do you want employees to meet expectations, or do you want your employees to feel motivated and have stronger performance? Do *you* want to meet expectations, or do you want to be one of the best managers they've ever had?

They already get service awards. Isn't that enough? Service awards are for undisputable milestones, for example, a work anniversary or a major event in the person's life. While service awards are nice to have, they have little connection to the organization's performance. There are exceptions in some organizations that create rituals and lively conversations around these awards that everyone looks forward to and enjoys, but that is rare. It would be a disservice to the organization, to you, and to the employee to consider the service award a major form of recognition. Keep the service awards if that is a wonderful tradition in your organization; be sure, though, to separate it from authentic recognition, which can have a deeper meaning and better results.

Diversity of heritage, age, culture, background—how do these tie in? The feeling of knowing your work has value and impact is universal. It is the approach we take that matters. In some cultures, public recognition is not desired; in others, it may be expected. From an age standpoint, generally speaking, we do know that Millennials, otherwise known as Generation Y (ages 20s to mid-30s), who will soon make up the majority of the workforce, have a higher expectation for feedback. They also like to know that others are aware that they've been recognized. However, do not assume that all Millennials prefer public recognition. Regardless of age, heritage, culture, or background, look at your team as individuals and learn from each person and their preferences. This goes a long way in getting it right.

Do I need to change my recognition program or committee? The principles presented here will complement the successes within existing recognition programs and will help you identify parts that are lackluster. For example, employees thrive when their managers routinely reinforce the impactfulness of employees' work; the TIPSS easily address this important aspect, typically absent from traditional recognition approaches. Also, recognition committees can strategically focus less on finding creative ideas, encouraging peer-to-peer recognition, and so on and more on providing productive, sustainable recognition, advocating for recognition training for managers, and building these concepts into existing systems.

Appreciation

Developing this book has been a team effort from the beginning, and it is with deep appreciation that I share in this effort with each of you.

My husband Dan, for your unwavering support, creative ideas, skills for thinking broadly, and zeroing in on details. I am also so thankful for your ensuring that we remember to celebrate the important milestones.

My children, Olivia, Ben, and Simon. Your love for learning and intrinsic motivation inspired me throughout this book. No one keeps it more real than you, and I love you for that.

Jean Roessler, my first manager who modeled employee recognition straight from the heart. I am constantly learning from you.

Mazie Colen, for showing how authentic recognition is done. You give far more than you take, and your sheer talent and incredible personality still make me want to run a mile after talking with you!

Chris Schreiber, truly you wrote the book before it was written. I can't thank you enough for your influence.

Melissa Peltier, for your inspiration, support, creativity, and help with character development. So happy to have you as my early phase partner.

Tiffany Cavegn, for lighting the fire and adding your expertise to the process. I am eternally grateful for seizing that conversation with you.

Lori Hughes, for being my safety zone and helping ground the conversations with your wicked smart and practical expertise and sky-high standards. You are an amazing editor and awesome neighbor and friend. I am so grateful. This truly could not have happened without you.

Sheila Jenniges, for being my researcher-in-a-pinch, always-doing-more-than-I-expected, safe-in-your-hands, and fourth-set-of-eyes! Your continuous encouragement was perfect!

Pete Nelson, for believing in the concepts, your idealism, and eagerly agreeing to beta test them with your team.

Steve Favilla, for those accountability check-ins. They were just right.

Lori Spangler, for your constant support, advice, resources, and paving the way.

To the following who have each made this book uniquely better with their perspective:

Nancy Jenniges, for perfect suggestions on what's realistic and applying the concepts for plausibility, and for your positive support and eagerness to help.

Judy McDonald, one of my earliest supporters and champions, and my bounce-ideas-person at all odd times. I'm grateful for your endless, unique, and explicit insight.

Krishnapriya Nair, for helping me see what was missing and what was solid and for your HR perspective and pure joy for my process.

Diane Allen, for your executive perspective, experience, and invitation to go back to the well more than once.

Byron Bruce, for your conversation, gut check, and wisdom on service awards.

Helen Donnay, for your professional, articulate, right-on words of advice. Also for helping me consider the managers who don't see the expertise right in front of them.

Sarah Enoch, for eagerly volunteering to beta read, for your insightful feedback on the style, and for being a perfect benchmark to me.

Jen Esnough, for putting the concepts to immediate application and sharing your positive experiences on recognition.

Cheryl Jones, for carving out the time, your encouragement, honesty, and your executive HR perspective. It meant so much and was truly helpful and priceless.

Kyle Nelson, for drawing on your vast business book consumption, and for your fresh, direct, and very impactful feedback. Here's to a 5!

Geoff Thompson, for your philosophical, artistic, and technical perspective. Who else can do that? Your support has been so helpful and unique.

Daniel Wilt, for your encouragement and for reminding me it would happen at the right time. Your tough questions were so valuable.

Narendra Reddy, for inspiring the highly innovative and crazy-smart main characters.

Tim Jopek, for your conversations with Helen and looking closely at the concepts.

Renita McBride, you start with support and questions and obstacles come later. I adore that.

Marsh Danielson, for your encouragement, interest, and leadership gut check.

Mae Paluck, for your support, analytical thoughts, and sentimental reminders.

Alan Law, for engaging the recognition conversations often and keeping it lively, smart, interesting, and so much fun.

Green Bay Packaging team: Steve Danielson, Travis Ehlenfeldt, Scott Lindenfelser, Mike Mikrut, Brandon Roster, Rick Setts, Greg Twedt, Kris Urbach, Chris Vanseth, Lee Everson, and Steve Joeckel, for being game, trying the concepts, and supporting my Big Idea.

Ryan Bramble, for being a great benchmark against the concepts.

David Zetah, for your interest and our conversation.

Meryl Steinhauser, for your marketing savvy, advice, connections, and kindness.

Michelle Fairbanks, for so responsively sharing your design talent, wisdom, and guidance.

Liz Thompson, for your editing and insight.

Julie Grady, for your keen eye and sharp proofing skills. You were a critical part of the team.

And, for enriching my life in countless ways, Elaine and Alphonse Jenniges; the late Ervin and Loretta Dohmeier; Susie and Steve Stewart; Arden Hegland; Sherri and Terry Zetah; Cindy and Scott Zetah; Tony Jenniges; Randy and Connie Jenniges; Cathy and Byron Bruce; Mark and Jan Dohmeier; Deb and Jim Sater; Brandon, Aaron, Veronica, Andy, Dan, Kadin, Maddie, Axel, Jase, and Jackson Janachovsky; Mathias and Jeri McDonald; Zac, Amanda, Melissa, and Korey Zetah; Heather and Anthony Maule; Mason, Kyle, and Colby Zetah; Tyler and Ashley Jenniges; Alex, Taeler, and Emma Jenniges; Shannon and John Bruce; Jacob and Matthew Dohmeier; Sarah, Miranda, and Abby Sater; Ked Cordero; Kathy Curry, Dante, and Tom Pietrzak; Lorie Sollenberger, Ava, Lucas, and Rich Donato; Grayson Hughes; Sandy Law; Megan and Loren Moore; Jennifer Horrocks; Elizabeth Walker; Tom Kramlik; Michael Berger; Chuck Hanson; Mary Schmid;

Mark Murphy; the CRISP team; Erin Perdu; Niki and Pete Zug-schwert; Sara and Shawn Bromeland; Carlise Stembridge; Molly Steffek; Susan Scanlon; Luann Cosgrove; Pam and Bob Byers; Jen and Lucia Wroblewski; Jim Chase; Patty Shade; Glen Jones; Amanda Cade; and the AMI Montessori community and philosophy of the so-very-important concept of intrinsic motivation.

For those mentioned and those I may have missed, I know it is never too late to recognize how you have helped shape my journey. Thank you for adding to my life!

Notes

1. Achor, Shawn. *The Happiness Advantage: The Seven Principles That Fuel Success and Performance at Work*. New York: Crown Publishing Group, 2010.

2. "Report: State of the American Workplace." *Gallup.com*, September 22, 2014, http://www.gallup.com/services/176708/state-american-workplace.aspx

3. Robinson, Jennifer. "Be Nice: It's Good for Business." *Gallup.com Business Journal*, August 12, 2004, http://www.gallup.com/businessjournal/12577/nice-its-good-business.aspx

4. Mann, Annamarie, and Dvorak, Nate. "Employee Recognition: Low Cost, High Impact." *Gallup.com Business Journal*, June 28, 2016, http://www.gallup.com/businessjournal/193238/employee-recognition-low-cost-highimpact.aspx?g_source=employees%20who%20do%20not%20feel%20adequately%20recognized%20ar&g_medium=search&g_campaign=tiles

5. *The Power of Employee Recognition*. The Aberdeen Group, November 2013, http://go.globoforce.com/rs/globoforce/images/AberdeenReportNovember2013.pdf

6. Bersin, Josh. "New Research Unlocks the Secret of Employee Recognition." *Forbes.com*, June 13, 2013. https://www.forbes.com/sites/joshbersin/2012/06/13/new-research-unlocks-the-secret-of-employee-recognition/#697495cd5276

7. Adkins, Amy. "Employee Engagement in U.S. Stagnant in 2015." *Gallup.com*, January 13, 2016, http://www.gallup.com/poll/188144/employee-engagement-stagnant-2015.aspx?g_source=engaged&g_medium=search&g_campaign=tiles

8. Mann, Annamarie, and Harter, Jim. "The Worldwide Employee Engagement Crisis." *Gallup.com Business Journal*, January 7, 2016, http://news.gallup.com/businessjournal/188033/worldwide-employee-engagement-crisis.aspx

9. O'Brien, John, and Shuck, Brad. "Workplace Trends That Will Affect Your 2015 Employee Engagement Strategy." http://www.biworldwide.co.uk/globalassets/en-gb/research-materials1/white-papers/bi-worldwide_employee_workplace-trends_uk.pdf

10. Garr, Stacia. "The State of Employee Recognition 2012." Bersin by Deloitte, June 11, 2012, https://www.bersin.com/Practice/Detail.aspx?id=15539

11. Beck, Randall, and Harter, Jim. "Managers Account for 70% of Variance in Employee Engagement." *Gallup.com Business Journal*, April 21, 2015, http://www.gallup.com/businessjournal/182792/managers-account-variance-employee-engagement.aspx

12. Dewhurst, Martin, Guthridge, Matthew, and Mohr, Elizabeth. "Motivating People, Getting Beyond Money." *McKinsey Quarterly*, November 2009, http://www.mckinsey.com/business-functions/organization/our-insights/motivating-people-getting-beyond-money)

About Work with Clients

As an Organizational Development and Leadership Training consultant for more than 20 years, Sam (Sandra) K. Jenniges loves to partner with clients to develop and retain exceptional performers to help organizations reach their full potential. Working with all organizational levels, she is known for building the desired culture and for perpetually inspiring employees and organizations to be their very best. Areas of specialty include recognition, leadership development, culture building, onboarding programs, employee surveys, and customized training programs.

Sam has worked with Fortune 500 companies, small and mid-size firms, universities, and healthcare organizations. Some of her clients include Microsoft Corporation, Campbell's, and Penn State University.

To learn about how Sam can be a resource for you, please contact her:

contact@samjenniges.com
www.samjenniges.com

The *Recognition Rebooted* Training Program

Think differently and more simply about employee recognition. Human Resources professionals and managers have been unfairly expected to be "naturals" and experts in employee recognition. Intentions are good, yet critical opportunities are missed and time, energy, and money are wasted. Rather than sincere recognition, meaningless rewards and one-size-fits-all public recognition are too often given, falling flat and sometimes even demotivating employees. It's time to change that! The *Recognition Rebooted* interactive training session helps managers get good at delivering employee recognition. In addition, these principles will complement existing recognition program components that are working well and will provide tools to help quickly reboot the practices that are lackluster. Participants will learn how to

- Deliberately and strongly influence the way employees feel about their jobs
- Easily deliver recognition in a very targeted way
- Effectively motivate teams to give their full effort, love their work, and stay with the company

This session is highly interactive, eye-opening, and engaging. All Human Resources professionals and managers of employees will benefit from the program, regardless of whether their organizations have an existing recognition program. It's time to do better.

contact@samjenniges.com
www.samjenniges.com

About the Author

Sam Jenniges, M.S., grew up on a farm in southwestern Minnesota as the fourth of eight children in her family. Farm life helped her learn quickly that a little appreciation for work well done can increase performance no matter how unappealing the job is! She graduated from the University of Minnesota with a BA degree in Scientific and Technical Communications and from St. Joseph's University in Philadelphia with an MS degree in Organizational Development and Leadership.

Sam's early career began on a team of organizational development practitioners who helped their IT consulting firm differentiate from industry peers through a strong values-based culture. This enabled recruitment of exceptional performers as well as employee and client retention. Career highlights include developing organizational development and leadership certifications, creating a simulation board game (patent pending) used in a major university's IT curriculum, developing world-class onboarding and masters programs, and dozens of customized leadership and training programs.

Sam resides in White Bear Lake, Minnesota, with her husband and three children. She enjoys traveling with her family, cooking, paddle-boarding, cross-country skiing, and yes, the Minnesota winters.

CPSIA information can be obtained
at www.ICGtesting.com
Printed in the USA
BVHW031611191119
564177BV00006B/469/P